A KID'S UPCYCLING GUIDE TO CRAFTS

trash to treasure

Fun, Easy Projects with Paper, Plastic, Glass & Ceramics, Fabric, Metal, and Odds & Ends

PAM SCHEUNEMANN

SCARLETTA JUNIOR READERS

MINNEAPOLIS, MINNESOTA

W9-AYN-041

Copyright © 2013 Scarletta
Published by Scarletta Junior Readers, an imprint of Scarletta
This book is a collaborative arrangement between Scarletta and
ABDO Publishing Company. All rights reserved. No part of this
book may be used or reproduced in any manner whatsoever
without written permission except in the case of brief quotations
embodied in critical articles and reviews. For information, write
to Scarletta, 10 South Fifth Street #1105, Minneapolis, MN
55402, U.S.A., www.scarlettapress.com.

The Lexile Framework for Reading®
Lexile Measure® 590L
LEXILE®, LEXILE FRAMEWORK®, LEXILE ANALYZER® and
the LEXILE® logo are trademarks of MetaMetrics, Inc.,
and are registered in the United States and abroad. The
trademarks and names of other companies and
products mentioned herein are the property of their
respective owners. Copyright © 2011 MetaMetrics, Inc.
All rights reserved.

Library of Congress Cataloging-in-Publication Data
Scheunemann, Pam, 1955-
  Trash to treasure : a kid's upcycling guide to crafts / by Pam
Scheunemann. -- First edition.
     pages cm
  Audience: 9+
  Audience: Grade 4 to 6.
  Summary: "With easy step-by-step instructions, this book will
help kids get creative and recycle and repurpose their trash
into handmade treasures. All projects feature common everyday
items to reuse in a fun new way. From bottle-top pop art to
felted tin-can organizers, kids will love making useful crafts
and helping the environment. Great tips and advice on reusing,
garage sales, and spotting treasures are also provided. So start
your upcycling with these fabric, paper, metal, glass & ceramics,
and odds & ends projects. Book includes: visual supply & tool
lists, step-by-step instructions and photos, fun advice & tips,
and safety information"-- Provided by publisher.
  ISBN 978-1-938063-18-3 (pbk.) -- ISBN 978-1-938063-19-0
(electronic)
  1. Handicraft--Juvenile literature. 2. Recycling (Waste,
etc.)--Juvenile literature. 3. Salvage (Waste, etc.)--Juvenile
literature. I. Title.
  TT160.S2973 2013
  745.5--dc23
                                       2013010144
  ISBN-13 978-1-938063-18-3 (pbk. : alk. paper)
  ISBN-13 978-1-938063-19-0 (electronic)

Design by Mighty Media Inc., Minneapolis, MN
Cover design and interior production by Colleen Dolphin
Interior design by Anders Hanson

The following manufacturers/names appearing in this book
are trademarks: 3M™ Scotch®, Aleene's® Tacky Glue®,
Americana® Multi-Purpose™ Sealer, Arrow®, Artist's
Loft™, Avery®, Connoisseur Carnival, Craft Smart®, Creative
Imaginations®, DMC®, DoubleTree by Hilton™, Elmer's®,
Fiskars®, Glitter Glue™, Goo Gone®, Krylon®, Marvy®
DecoColor™, Mod Podge®, NYC New York Color®, Painter's
Mate Green®, Quick Grip™, Rapala®, Reynolds®, Rust-oleum®,
Sanford®, Scrabble®, Sharpie®, Singer®, Soft n Crafty®,
Sunbeam®, Tulip® Soft Fabric Paint™, Up & Up™, Weldbond®,
Westcott™

Printed and Manufactured in the United States
Distributed by Publishers Group West
First edition
10 9 8 7 6 5 4 3 2 1

TABLE OF CONTENTS

trash to treasure

Get into upcycling! Upcycling is making useful and cool things out of materials that might otherwise be discarded. Find potential treasures in garbage cans and recycling bins. Help save the earth by creating less trash. This book will show you how to make upcycling fun.

Using upcycling to create art has tons of benefits. You can help the planet. You can make cool stuff for yourself. You can create awesome gifts for your family and friends. You can even save useful things from going into the trash heap. And the best part is you don't have to spend a lot of money doing it.

Permission and Safety

- Always get permission before making any type of craft at home.
- Ask if you can use the tools and materials needed.
- Ask for help when you need it.
- Be careful when using knives, scissors, or other sharp objects.
- Be especially careful if you happen to break any glass.

Be Prepared

- Read the entire activity before you begin.
- Make sure you have everything you need to do the project.
- Keep your work area clean and organized.
- Follow the directions carefully.
- Clean up after you are finished for the day.

In this book, you'll find great ideas to upcycle materials such as paper, plastic, glass, ceramics, fabric, metal, and other odds and ends. Each section in the book is all about reusing a different type of material. Make them just as they appear in the book or get creative using your own ideas.

There are endless ways that you can make something beautiful and useful from discarded materials. This book will help you get started. When you're done, be sure to keep an eye out for hidden gems around your house and at garage sales and thrift stores. The sky's the limit!

TOOLS & MATERIALS

1/8-INCH (3 MM) HEAVY DUTY HOLE PUNCH

ACRYLIC PAINT

ADDRESS LABELS

ADHESIVE LETTERS

ALL-PURPOSE SEALER

ARTIST'S CANVAS

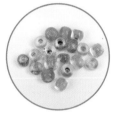

BEADS

BROWN PAPER BAG

BUTTONS

CARD STOCK

CARDBOARD

CD JEWEL CASE

CERAMIC VASE & CANDLE HOLDERS

CHAIN NECKLACE

CHALK

CHALKBOARD PAINT

Here are some of the things that you'll need to get started!

CIRCLE PUNCH

CLEAR FISHING LINE

COASTER-SIZE TILES

COLORED TISSUE PAPER

COLORED WIRE

COLORFUL FLAT MARBLES

COMPUTER KEYBOARD

CONTACT PAPER

COPPER PIPE

COPPER PIPE CAP

CORK SHEET

COTTON CLOTHESLINE

CRAFT FELT

CRAFT KNIFE

CURTAIN ROD

DECORATIVE GEMS

DECORATIVE HOLE PUNCH

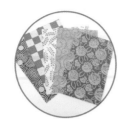

DECORATIVE PAPER

DECORATIVE-EDGE SCISSORS

DINNER KNIFE

DOMINOES AND/OR SCRABBLE TILES

DOUBLE-SIDED TAPE

DUCT TAPE

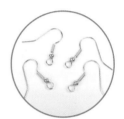

EAR WIRES

EARBUDS

EMBROIDERY FLOSS

EMBROIDERY NEEDLE

ENVELOPES

FABRIC PAINT

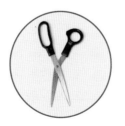

FABRIC SCISSORS

FABRIC SCRAPS

FLAT-NOSED PLIERS

FLORAL STEM WIRE

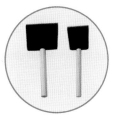

FOAM BRUSHES

FRAME

FRAME WITH GLASS

FREEZER PAPER

FROSTED GLASS PAINT

GLITTER GLUE

GLUE STICK

GLUE-ON BAILS

GREEN CHENILLE STEMS

GRILL

HANG RINGS

HEAD PINS

HOLE PUNCH

**HOT GLUE GUN
& GLUE STICKS**

ISOPROPYL ALCOHOL

JAR

JINGLE BELLS

JUMP RINGS

LABELS

LED VOTIVE LIGHTS

LOOSE-LEAF BOOK RINGS

LUCITE ROLLER

MAP

MARKER

MASKING TAPE

MEASURING TAPE

METAL SCREEN

METAL TRAY

MOD PODGE

MOD PODGE DIMENSIONAL MAGIC

NEEDLE-NOSED PLIERS

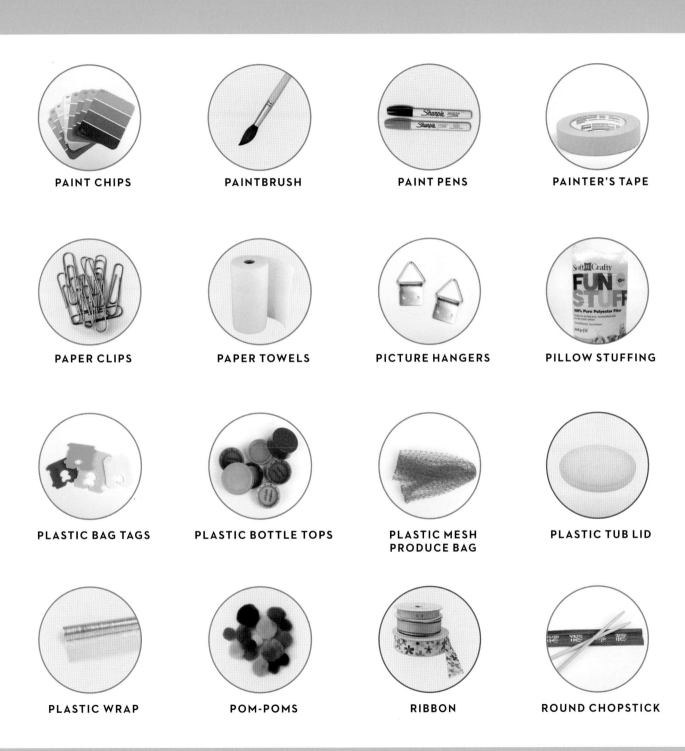

PAINT CHIPS	PAINTBRUSH	PAINT PENS	PAINTER'S TAPE
PAPER CLIPS	PAPER TOWELS	PICTURE HANGERS	PILLOW STUFFING
PLASTIC BAG TAGS	PLASTIC BOTTLE TOPS	PLASTIC MESH PRODUCE BAG	PLASTIC TUB LID
PLASTIC WRAP	POM-POMS	RIBBON	ROUND CHOPSTICK

ROUND MAGNETS

ROUND-NOSED PLIERS

RULER

RUSTY METAL PRIMER

SAFETY PINS

SANDING BLOCK

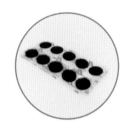

SELF-ADHESIVE HOOK-AND-LOOP DOTS

SODA CAN TABS

SPARKLE MOD PODGE

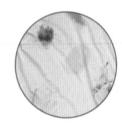

STAINED T-SHIRT

STICKERS

STIR STICK

STRAIGHT PINS

STRAIGHT-SIDED GLASS VASE

STURDY STAND

TACKY GLUE

TAG BOARD

TAPESTRY NEEDLES

TEACUP & SAUCER

TIES

TIN BOX

TIN CANS

TOGGLE CLASP

WAXED PAPER

WELDBOND

WIDE-EYE PLASTIC NEEDLE

WIRE

WIRE CUTTERS

WOODEN BEADS

WOODEN SKEWER

WOOL SWEATER

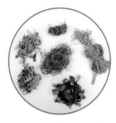

YARN SCRAPS

A FRESH LOOK AT PAPER

There are many sources of paper. Magazines, newspapers, junk mail, envelopes, greeting cards, candy wrappers, and wrapping paper are just a few. All of these types of paper can be upcycled. Here are some things you can make with unwanted paper.

Cards & Calendars

- PAPER EMBELLISHMENTS
- ENVELOPES
- NEW CARDS

Newspaper

- GIFT BAGS
- WRAPPING PAPER
- SEEDLING POTS

Magazines

- ENVELOPES
- BOWS
- **COLLAGES**

Maps

- PICTURE MATS
- ORIGAMI
- PAPER WEAVING

Tissue Paper

- DECOUPAGE
- PAPER FLOWERS
- BOWLS

STUFF YOU'LL NEED

- JAR WITH LID
- DECORATIVE PAPER
- MARKER
- RULER
- SCISSORS
- CARDBOARD
- MOD PODGE
- FOAM BRUSH

18

PAPER TOPPERS

Make cool lids in just a few minutes!

1   Wash and dry the lid and jar. Remove any labels. Find decorative paper that you like. It can be pieces of wrapping paper, **origami** paper, or scrapbook paper.

2   Put the lid upside down on the back of a piece of decorative paper. Trace a circle around it.

3   Measure the height of the sides of the lid. Double the measurement. Make several marks around the circle that distance away from it. Use the marks to draw a larger circle around the first circle. Cut out the larger circle.

4   Make cuts around the paper from the edge to the inner circle. Make them about ¼ inch (.6 cm) apart.

5   Brush Mod Podge over the inner circle. Press the jar lid on top of it. Turn it over and smooth out any wrinkles in the paper.

6   Place the lid on a piece of cardboard. Brush Mod Podge on a couple of the strips of paper. Fold the strips one at a time over the edge of the lid. Continue gluing and folding the remaining strips.

7   Turn the lid over. Cover the top and sides with Mod Podge. Let it dry completely before putting the lid back on the jar.

STUFF YOU'LL NEED

- DECORATIVE, COLORED, AND PLAIN PAPER SCRAPS

- RULER

- PENCIL

- SCISSORS

- GLUE STICK

- LUCITE ROLLER

- HOLE PUNCH

- 8-INCH (20-CM) RIBBON

WOVEN PAPER BOOKMARK

Makes a really cool design!

1. First you need to make a **template**. Start with a plain, 3-by-5-inch (6-by-10-cm) piece of paper. Fold it in half **lengthwise**.

2. Draw a straight line 1/2 inch (1 cm) from the fold. Draw another line 1 inch (2 cm) from the fold.

3. Make marks along the folded edge every 1/4 inch (.5 cm). Make the same marks along the 1-inch (2-cm) line.

4. Position the paper with the fold toward you. Start on the right side. Line the ruler up between the second mark on the 1-inch (2-cm) line and the corner of the fold. Draw a line from the 1-inch (2-cm) line to the corner.

5. Line the ruler up between the third mark on the 1-inch (2-cm) line and the first mark on the fold. Draw a line from the 1/2-inch (1-cm) line to the fold. Move the ruler so it is lined up between the fourth mark on the 1-inch (2-cm) line and the second mark on the fold. Draw a line from the 1-inch line to the fold. Keep moving the ruler and drawing lines, alternating between long and short lines. Stop when you get to the left side of the paper.

Continued on the next page

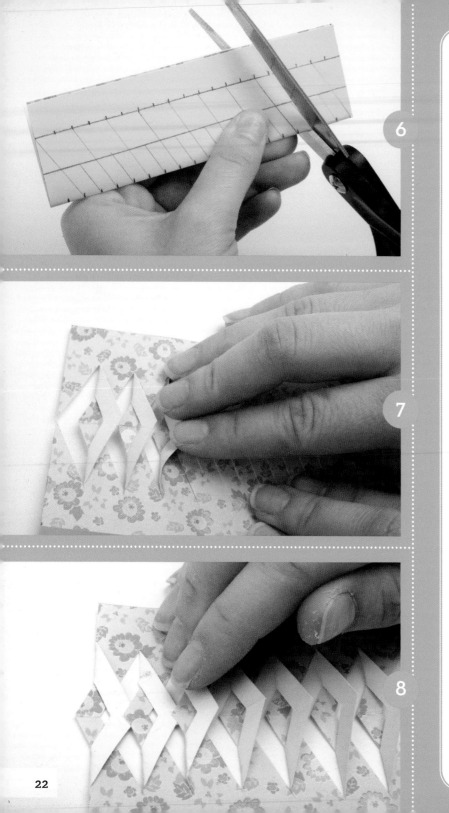

6   Cut a 3-by-5-inch (6-by-10-cm) piece of decorative paper. Fold it in half **lengthwise**. Wrap the fold of the **template** over the fold of the decorative paper. Cut on the **diagonal** lines.

7   Remove the template and unfold the decorative paper. Lay it down with the fold facing up. The diagonal cuts will form points. Carefully fold the wider points down. Crease the edges. Cut off any extra paper at the ends.

8   Use the glue stick to put a little glue on the tips of the points you folded down. Tuck them under the points facing the other way. Press each one firmly.

9   Cut a piece of colored paper a little larger than 3 by 5 inches (6 by 10 cm).

10   Use the glue stick to cover the back of the woven decorative paper with glue. Press it in the center of the colored paper. Roll over it with a Lucite roller.

11   Punch a hole at one end of the weaving.

12   Fold the ribbon in half. Push the fold through the hole from front to back. Wrap the ends over the top. Stick them through the fold in the ribbon.

STUFF YOU'LL NEED

- 5 ENVELOPES THAT ARE THE SAME SIZE

- GLUE STICK

- SCISSORS

- RIBBON

- LABELS

- MARKER

- STICKERS

- COLORED PAPER

ENVELOPE ORGANIZER

Wrap up your paper bits in this!

1. Spread glue on the inside of one envelope flap. Lay the second envelope on top of it. Press firmly. Spread glue on the flap of that envelope. Lay the third envelope on top of it. Press firmly. Add the fourth envelope the same way.

2. Make small cuts in the top and bottom of the fifth envelope. The cuts should be as wide as the ribbon. Push the ribbon through both cuts.

3. Spread glue on the outside of the fourth envelope's flap. Press it onto the pocket of the fifth envelope. Let the glue dry.

4. Write the content of each envelope on the labels. Stick a label on the pocket of each envelope. Decorate the envelopes with stickers and bits of colored paper.

5. Fold the envelopes **accordion**-style and tie the ribbon around them. Or use the ribbon to hang them up as a wall organizer.

- ENVELOPE

- MAP

- MARKER

- SCISSORS

- RULER

- DINNER KNIFE

- GLUE STICK

- WHITE ADDRESS
  LABELS

MaP-VELOPE

Help your cards find their way!

1. Carefully open up the envelope along the seams. Unfold it completely.

2. Lay the envelope on the map. Trace around the envelope. Cut it out just inside the lines, so they won't show. Lay the map cutout face down on the table.

3. Look at where the folds are in the envelope you traced. You'll need to fold your map envelope the same way. Place the ruler where you want to make a fold. Run the back of a dinner knife along the ruler. This **scores** the paper where you will fold it. Continue to score the map everywhere it needs to be folded.

4. Fold in the side flaps. Put glue along both edges of the bottom flap. Fold the bottom flap up and press it to the side flaps. Let the glue dry.

5. When you are ready to mail something, put it in the envelope and glue the top flap down. Use labels to add the mailing address and your return address.

STUFF YOU'LL NEED

- NEWSPAPER
- ARTIST'S CANVAS
- ACRYLIC PAINT
- FOAM BRUSH
- PAINT CHIPS
- CIRCLE PUNCH
- GLUE STICK

PAINT CHIP POP ART

Pop goes the easel!

1. Spread newspaper over your work surface. Paint the whole artist's **canvas**. Paint a couple of coats. Let the paint dry after each coat.

2. Use the circle punch to cut circles out of paint chips.

3. Arrange the paint chip circles on the canvas. Glue them down. Let the glue dry.

4. Find a great place to hang your art!

STUFF YOU'LL NEED

- **MAGAZINES**
- **SCISSORS**
- **RULER**
- **LARGE PAPER CLIPS**
- **GLUE STICK**
- **SPLIT RINGS**
- **CURTAIN ROD**

How Many Rings & Paper Clips?

Measure the width of the space where you will hang the curtain. You will need one split ring per 1 inch (2.5 cm). That is how many chains you will make.

Measure the height of the space. For each chain, you will need one paper clip per 2 inches (5 cm) in height.

SCRAP PAPER CURTAIN

Hang it in a doorway or window!

1 Find some colorful magazine pages. Cut out rectangles that are 1$\frac{1}{2}$ by 2 inches (4 by 5 cm). You will need a rectangle for each paper clip.

2 Push a short side of one of the rectangles under the middle of a paper clip.

3 Wrap the paper all the way around the paper clip. Make sure the side you want to show is facing out. Run the glue stick under the edge of the paper. Press it down firmly.

4 Attach another paper clip to the first paper clip. Wrap it with a paper rectangle the same way you did the first one. Keep adding paper clips and wrapping them with paper. Stop when the chain is as long as the height of the space where you will hang it.

5 Repeat steps 2 through 4 to make a chain for each split ring. Attach a split ring to one end of each chain. Put the split rings on the curtain rod. You may need to have an adult help you hang the curtain rod.

- **MAGAZINES**
- **ROUND CHOPSTICK**
- **GLUE STICK**
- **WOODEN SKEWER**
- **SCISSORS**
- **OLD FRAME**
- **FOAM BRUSH**
- **MOD PODGE**

Magazine Roll Frame

Upcycle an old frame!

1. Find some colorful magazine pages. Look for pages with outer edges that have colors you like. Rip out the pages.

2. Lay a page down with the colored edge you like face down. Set the chopstick on the torn edge of the page. Use the glue stick to put a line of glue slightly in front of the chopstick.

3. Roll the page tightly around the chopstick. Put glue along the end of the paper. Press it to the roll. Use the wooden skewer to push the chopstick out of the roll of paper.

4. Repeat steps 2 and 3 to make more colorful rolls of paper. Let the glue dry.

5. Remove the backing and glass from the frame. Cut the paper rolls into pieces and arrange them on the frame. Cover the frame completely with rolls of paper. Glue the rolls onto the frame. Let the glue dry.

6. Cover the frame with a couple of coats of Mod Podge. Let it dry after each coat. Then add your favorite photo!

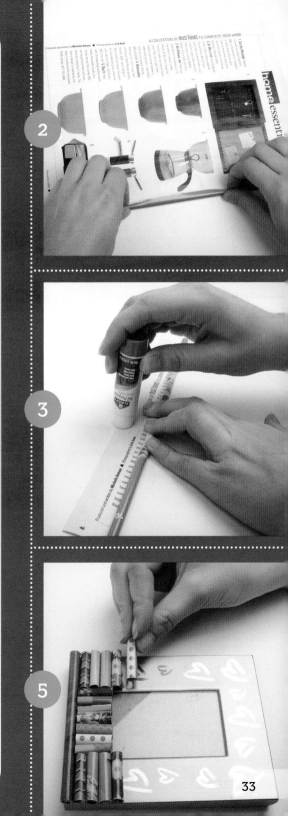

STUFF YOU'LL NEED

- NEWSPAPER
- BOWL
- PLASTIC WRAP
- MASKING TAPE
- JAR
- FOAM BRUSH
- MOD PODGE
- WHITE RECYCLED PAPER
- SANDING BLOCK
- PAPER TOWEL
- SCISSORS
- ACRYLIC PAINT
- FOAM BRUSH
- MARKERS OR PAINT PENS
- ALL-PURPOSE SEALER

PAINTED PAPER BOWL

Turn newspaper into a bowl!

1. Spread newspaper over your work surface. Cover the outside of the bowl with plastic wrap.

2. Pull the plastic wrap so it is as smooth as possible. Tape the edges to the inside of the bowl.

3. Place the bowl upside down on top of the jar. Make sure the jar is tall enough that the bowl doesn't touch the table. Tear newspaper into strips.

4. Brush Mod Podge on the bowl. Brush a little Mod Podge on a newspaper strip. Stick the strip to the bowl. Brush Mod Podge over the strip. Keep adding Mod Podge and strips of newspaper until the bowl is covered. Let it dry for an hour. Add two more layers of Mod Podge and newspaper strips. Let it dry for an hour between each layer.

Continued on the next page

5. Put on a final layer of paper and Mod Podge. This time use white paper instead of newspaper. There can be writing on one side of the white paper. Just stick the printed side to the bowl. Let the bowl dry for at least nine hours.

6. Use the sanding block to smooth out any rough spots. Don't rub too hard or you'll wear the surface down. Wipe the bowl with a damp paper **towel** to get rid of the dust.

7. Remove the tape from the plastic wrap. Gently remove both bowls from the plastic wrap.

8 Trim around the edge of the paper bowl to even it out. Or just leave it as is for a rougher look.

9 Paint the bowl white. Let it dry.

10 Paint the inside of the bowl with colored paint. Add some cool shapes. Let it dry. Outline the shapes with a black marker or paint pen.

11 Put the bowl upside down on the jar. Paint the outside of the bowl. Let the paint dry completely. You can use the same color as the inside or a different color. Paint some more shapes. Let it dry. Use paint pens or markers to add other decorations.

12 Cover the bowl with a coat of all-purpose sealer. Let it dry completely.

This bowl is not safe to serve food in, unless the food is wrapped so it doesn't touch the bowl.

A FRESH LOOK AT PLASTIC

Many everyday items are made out of plastic. Plastic can be found all around us. And recycling is not an option for many types of plastic. Here are some ideas for reusing or upcycling plastic.

Plastic Bottles

- FLOWER POTS
- VASES
- PIGGY BANK OR CHANGE JAR

Bread Bag Tags

- LABELS FOR ELECTRIC CORDS, SPARE KEYS, AND GARDEN PLANTS
- USE ONE TO MARK THE END OF A ROLL OF TAPE

Gift Cards & Credit Cards

- CABLE/CORD ORGANIZER
- JEWELRY
- COASTERS
- GUITAR PICKS

Mesh Produce Bags

- SOAP HOLDER
- POT SCRUBBER
- VEGETABLE SCRUBBER
- REUSEABLE PRODUCE BAG
- BAG FOR CONTAINER LIDS

CD Jewel Cases

- PICTURE FRAMES
- DISPLAY FOR A BUTTERFLY COLLECTION
- DESKTOP CALENDAR STAND
- COASTERS

Plastic Buttons

- MAGNETS
- JEWELRY
- GREETING CARD DECORATIONS

STUFF YOU'LL NEED

- **PLASTIC BUTTONS WITH HOLES**
- **MARKER**
- **PAPER**
- **SCISSORS**
- **CRAFT FELT**
- **CLEAR TAPE**
- **FLORAL STEM WIRE**
- **GREEN CHENILLE STEMS**
- **GLITTER GLUE**
- **DECORATIVE GEMS**
- **VASE**

BUTTON BOUQUET

A great way to reuse buttons!

1. Make stacks of two or three buttons that look good together.

2. Draw circles and flower shapes on a piece of paper. Make them different sizes. Cut them out.

3. Select colors of felt that go with the buttons. Roll up a piece of tape and put it on a paper shape. Stick the paper shape to the felt. Cut around the paper shape. Use the paper shapes to cut out more felt shapes.

Continued on the next page

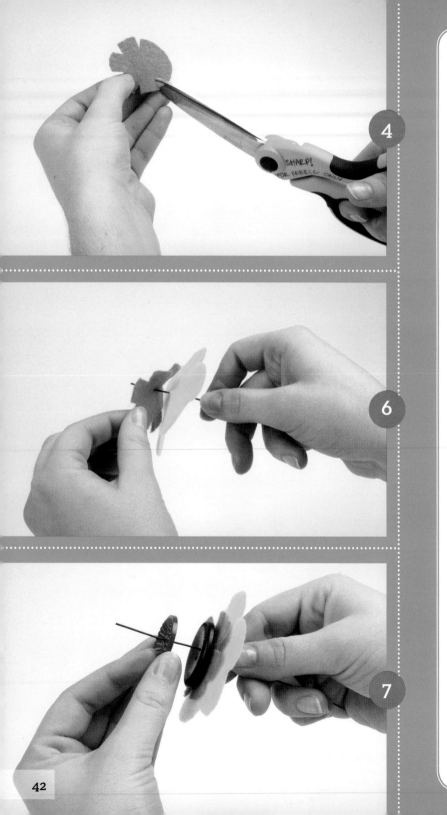

4 You can cut little triangles into the felt circles to make flowers.

5 Stack the buttons on top of the felt shapes. Try different combinations of felt and buttons. Rearrange them until you like the way they look.

6 Choose one stack to start with. Poke a piece of floral stem wire up through the center of the bottom felt shape. Then poke it through any other felt shapes in the stack.

7 Stick the wire through a hole in each button.

8. Bend the wire and push it back through the buttons. Use different holes in the buttons.

9. Push the buttons up to the bend in the wire. Poke the wire back through the felt. Pull tight so the buttons are against the felt. Twist the ends of the wire together to make one stem.

10. Twist the end of the chenille stem around the wire just under the felt. Wrap the chenille stem around the wire stem.

11. Decorate the felt with glitter glue and decorative gems.

12. Repeat steps 6 through 11 to make more button flowers. Put them in a vase!

- **PLASTIC BAG TAGS, DIFFERENT SIZES**

- **1/8-INCH HEAVY-DUTY HOLE PUNCH**

- **ACRYLIC PAINT**

- **PAINTBRUSH**

- **PAINT PENS**

- **ALL-PURPOSE SEALER**

- **DECORATIVE GEMS**

- **CRAFT GLUE**

- **JUMP RINGS**

- **CHAIN NECKLACE**

- **FLAT-NOSED PLIERS**

- **TOGGLE CLASP**

BAG TAG NECKLACE

You'll look fresh in this beauty!

1. Punch a hole in one corner of 14 small bag tags. Put the hole in the same spot on all the tags. Punch holes in two corners of a large bag tag.

2. Paint one side of each tag white. Let the paint dry. Then paint the other side white. Let the paint dry. Then paint each tag with a color. Do one side and then the other. Let the paint dry between sides. It will take a few coats of paint to cover the tags well.

3. Use paint pens to decorate the tags. Don't forget to do both sides. Let the paint dry between sides. Put a coat of all-purpose sealer on both sides of each tag. Let it dry. Then glue on some decorative gems. Let the glue dry.

4. Put a jump ring through the hole in a tag. Then put it through a link in the chain. Hold one side of the jump ring with the flat-nosed pliers. Twist the ring so the ends line up. Attach all of the small tags to the chain this way. Attach the large tag in the middle using two jump rings. Arrange the tags any way you want!

5. Decide how long you want the **necklace** to be. Use the pliers to remove any extra links from the chain. Add a toggle clasp to join the ends together.

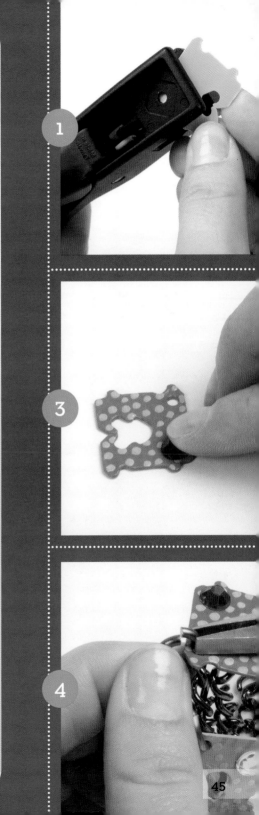

45

STUFF YOU'LL NEED

- CD JEWEL CASE
- CARD STOCK
- RULER
- SCISSORS
- CRAFT GLUE
- PHOTO OR ARTWORK
- RIBBON
- DECORATIVE PAPER
- DECORATIVE GEMS

JEWEL CASE FRAME

A good case for upcycling!

1. Open the CD case. Snap out the tray that holds the CD. Remove all paper and labels from the jewel case. Wash and dry it.

2. Cut a square piece of card stock that is 4³/4 inches (12 cm) on each side.

3. Glue the photo or artwork to the card stock. Decorate the card stock around the picture. You could glue on colorful paper, ribbon, or gems. Or think of your own ideas. Just make sure that the decorations don't stick out past the sides of the card stock.

4. Gently remove the lid of the jewel case. Flip the bottom of the case over. Reattach the lid. The lid should be propped up by the bottom.

5. Slip the card stock behind the tabs in the lid of the CD case. Make sure the picture is against the plastic so it faces out. If you like, you can add decorations to the outside of the frame too!

47

STUFF YOU'LL NEED

- PLASTIC MESH PRODUCE BAG
- SCISSORS
- RULER
- SAFETY PIN
- 36-INCH (91-CM) RIBBON
- PLASTIC TUB LID
- CRAFT KNIFE

BAG FOR THE BEACH

Sand won't mesh with this bag!

1. Cut the top of the mesh bag evenly. Fold the top in about 1 inch (2.5 cm).

2. Attach the safety pin to the end of the ribbon. Weave it in and out of the folded mesh. Go around the entire opening of the bag.

3. Stretch the bag open as wide as you can. Tie the ends of the ribbon together.

4. Have an adult help you use a craft knife to cut a small X in the center of the plastic lid. Put the lid inside the bag.

5. Push a little bit of the bottom of the bag through the X. If there is a metal tab on the bag, push it through the X. It will keep the bag from falling back out. If there is no metal tab, tie a knot in the part of the bag you pushed through the X.

49

Keyboard
Journal
(page 53)

Keyboard
Calendar
(pages
51–52)

STUFF YOU'LL NEED

- OLD COMPUTER KEYBOARD

- FLAT-HEAD SCREWDRIVER

- NEEDLE-NOSED PLIERS

- SMALL PAINTBRUSH

- CHALKBOARD PAINT

- ACRYLIC PAINT

- COMPUTER & PRINTER

- COLORED PAPER

- STAR-SHAPED HOLE PUNCH

- MOD PODGE

- HOT GLUE GUN & GLUE STICKS

- ROUND MAGNETS

- CHALK

- CARDBOARD

- JOURNAL WITH A PLAIN COVER

- RULER

- PENCIL

Keyboard Calendar

Let these bright keys count the days!

1. Use a flat-head screwdriver to **pry** the keys out of the keyboard. You will need 31 keys the same size plus the space bar.

2. Wash the keys with soap and water. If there is anything sticking out of the backs of the keys, pull it off with the pliers. Make sure the back of each key is flat.

3. Paint the space bar with chalkboard paint. Let it dry.

4. Paint the tops and sides of the other keys with acrylic paint. It will take a few coats of paint. Let the paint dry between each coat.

5. Type the numbers 1 through 31 on a computer. Space them out on the page in rows and columns. Print out the page on colored paper. Cut out each column of numbers. Cut the columns wide enough that the star hole punch can fit over the numbers.

Continued on the next page

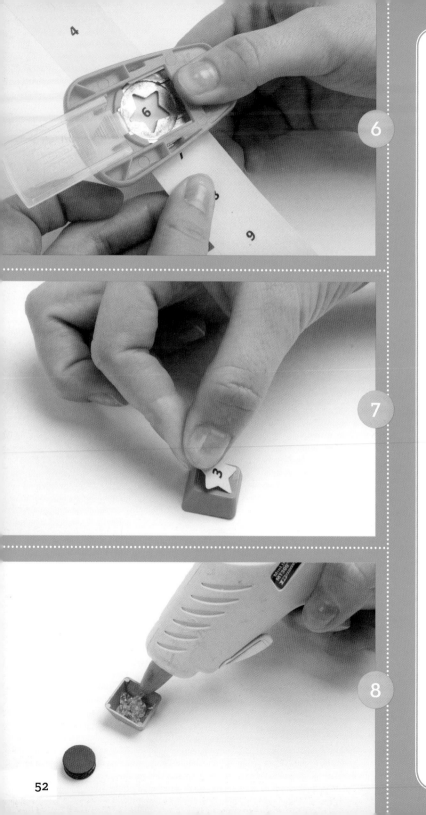

6 Center the star-shaped hole punch over each number. Punch out the numbers.

7 Paint the top of a key with Mod Podge. Gently press a star number on top. If it sticks over the edge, just press the points down. Brush a coat of Mod Podge over the whole key. Glue the other 30 star numbers to keys the same way. Let the Mod Podge dry completely.

8 Have an adult help you use the hot glue gun. Glue a magnet to the back of each key. Try to keep the magnets even with the backs of the keys. Glue two magnets to the back of the space bar. Let the glue dry completely.

9 Put the magnets on the refrigerator or other metal surface. Write the current month on the space bar with chalk. Arrange the days of the month underneath it.

KEYBOARD JOURNAL

The cover is key!

1. Use a flat-head screwdriver to **pry** the keys out of the keyboard. Wash the keys with soap and water. If there is anything sticking out of the backs of the keys, pull it off with the pliers. Make sure the back of each key is flat.

2. On a piece of cardboard, arrange the keys the way you want them to go on the journal cover. Make sure the arrangement is smaller than the journal.

3. Measure the size of your arrangement. Mark an area that size on the journal cover in pencil.

4. Have an adult help you use the hot glue gun to glue the keys to the journal cover. Start in one corner. Make a square of glue the same size as a key. Press the key into the glue. Position it quickly before the glue hardens. Glue on the rest of the keys one at a time. Let the glue dry completely.

STUFF YOU'LL NEED

- SQUARE ARTIST'S CANVAS
- RULER
- PENCIL
- ACRYLIC PAINT
- PAINTBRUSH
- MARKER
- PLASTIC BOTTLE TOPS
- DECORATIONS
- CRAFT GLUE
- GLITTER GLUE

BOTTLE TOP POP ART

Take your art to the top!

1. Use a ruler and pencil to divide the **canvas** into squares. Make sure each square is at least as big as a bottle top.

2. Paint each of the squares a different color. When the paint is dry, use a fat marker to outline the squares.

3. Decorate the insides of the bottle tops. Glue on gems, buttons, foam, or whatever you like. Use your creativity and a lot of glitter glue!

4. Glue each bottle top inside one of the squares. Let the glue dry.

55

GLASS
AND·CERAMICS

Many everyday items are made of glass. Glass can be found all around us. It's in jars, bottles, plates, bowls, and more. Here are some ideas for reusing or upcycling glass and **ceramics**.

Glass Jars

Jars come in many sizes and colors. Here are some things they can be made into.

- VASES
- PIGGY BANKS OR CHANGE JARS
- STORAGE CONTAINERS
- CANDLE HOLDERS

Glassware and Ceramics

More than likely you have some unused glass items around your house. You can also go to garage sales and thrift stores. They often have a lot of glassware and ceramics. Some of it, such as vases, you may want to reuse as is. But you can also upcycle those pieces. There are some projects in this book that will show you how. Here are some things you can make.

- BIRD FEEDERS
- SERVING PLATES
- UNUSUAL PLANTERS

CLEANING THE GLASS

Glass jars often have labels that must be removed before you reuse them. Some labels come off easily and some take a bit more work. First wash the jar in hot, soapy water. Let it dry. If there is still glue on the jar, use Goo Gone to remove it. Sometimes it is hard to get off. Just have patience and keep at it. Wash the jar again in hot, soapy water.

- COLORED TISSUE PAPER

- DECORATIVE-EDGE SCISSORS

- STRAIGHT-SIDED GLASS VASE

- MOD PODGE

- FOAM BRUSH

- CARD STOCK

- DECORATIVE HOLE PUNCHES

Save tissue paper from gifts you receive. You can reuse it in projects such as this one.

ALL WRAPPED UP

Makes a great candle holder or vase!

1. Crumple a piece of tissue paper. Then smooth it out. Fold it several times in the same direction. Use decorative-edge scissors to cut off the ends. Then cut along the folded edges.

2. Separate the strips of tissue paper. Cut the strips so that they fit around the vase. Make enough strips to cover the whole vase. Try using different colors.

3. Turn the vase upside down. Brush Mod Podge around the outside of the vase. Cover an area as wide as one of the tissue strips.

4. Wrap a strip around the vase over the Mod Podge. Smooth out any bubbles. It's okay if there are wrinkles. Spread more Mod Podge and add another strip below the first one. The strips should overlap a little bit. Repeat until the vase is covered with tissue paper. Let the Mod Podge dry.

5. Fold a piece of tissue paper into several layers. Put a piece of card stock behind the tissue paper to keep it stiff. Use a decorative hole punch to make small shapes.

6. Glue the shapes onto the vase. Let the Mod Podge dry. Then cover the whole vase with another coat of Mod Podge. Let it dry.

STUFF YOU'LL NEED

- CARD STOCK
- MARKER
- SCISSORS
- CONTACT PAPER
- SMALL GLASS JAR
- STICKERS & ADHESIVE LETTERS
- NEWSPAPER
- FROSTED GLASS PAINT
- LED VOTIVE LIGHT

Glass Jar Lantern

Fabulous, frosty, flickering flames!

1. Draw a design on the card stock. It can be anything you like. Make sure it will fit on the jar. Cut out the design. You will use it as a pattern.

2. Lay the pattern on the back side of the contact paper. Trace around the pattern. Cut it out.

3. Peel the backing off the contact-paper design. Stick the design on the jar. Add adhesive letters or other stickers.

4. Spread newspaper out in an area with good **ventilation**. It's best to do this outside or in a garage if you can. Set the jar upside down on the newspaper. Spray the jar with frosted glass paint. Follow the directions on the spray can.

5. Let the paint dry completely. Remove the contact paper and stickers. If there is a little glue left, gently rub it with a wet paper **towel**. Be careful not to scratch the paint. Put a votive light in the jar and enjoy the glow!

> Some stickers and contact paper are harder to remove than others. Test them on a different jar to make sure they will come off.

STUFF YOU'LL NEED

- GLASS JAR
- PAINTER'S TAPE
- NEWSPAPER
- CHALKBOARD PAINT
- STIR STICK
- FOAM BRUSH
- CHALK

REMARKABLE JAR

Change the label? No problem!

1. Use the painter's tape to make a border around the area you want to paint.

2. Spread newspaper over your work surface. Stir the paint. Paint the area inside the tape. Apply three coats. Let the paint dry between coats.

3. Let the last coat dry. Then carefully peel off the painter's tape.

4. Wait a few days to make sure the paint is completely dry. Then you can write on the painted area with chalk. Just erase the chalk when you need to change the label!

STUFF YOU'LL NEED

- COASTER-SIZE TILE
- RULER
- DECORATIVE PAPER OR PHOTO
- SCISSORS
- MOD PODGE
- FOAM BRUSH
- ACRYLIC SEALER
- CORK SHEET
- HOT GLUE GUN & GLUE STICKS

TERRIFIC TILE COASTER

Set your drinks on terrific tiles!

1. Measure the tile. Cut a piece of decorative paper or a photo 1/4 inch (.5 cm) smaller than the tile on each side.

2. Paint the top of the tile with Mod Podge.

3. Put the paper or photo in the center of the tile. Smooth out any air bubbles.

4. Brush Mod Podge over the paper or photo and all the way to the edges of the tile. Let it dry. Cover the tile with another coat of Mod Podge. Let it dry.

5. Put a coat of acrylic sealer on the tile. Let it dry.

6. Cut a piece of cork the same size you cut the paper or photo. Have an adult help you use the hot glue gun. Glue the cork to the back of the tile.

STUFF
YOU'LL
NEED

- GLASS JAR
- ACRYLIC PAINT
- RIBBON
- SCISSORS
- CRAFT GLUE
- GLITTER GLUE
- DECORATIVE GEMS

BOTTLE BLING

A creative container!

1. Pour acrylic paint into the jar. Gently swirl it around to cover the inside of the jar. Add more paint if necessary. When the entire inside of the jar is coated, pour out the extra paint. Let it dry.

2. Cut a piece of ribbon to fit around the jar. Glue the ribbon around the jar.

3. Lay the jar on its side. Put a dab of glitter glue on the jar. Press a gem into the glue. Add more gems to the side of the jar facing up. Let the glue dry. Then turn the jar to add gems to another side.

> Glitter glue takes a long time to dry. It can run if the jar is not lying flat.

STUFF YOU'LL NEED

- TEACUP & SAUCER
- SANDING BLOCK
- WELDBOND
- HEAVY BOOK
- METAL SPOON
- COPPER PIPE CAP
- COPPER PIPE, 4 FEET (1.2 M) LONG
- BIRDSEED

TEA TIME FOR BIRDS

Invite some birds to a tea party!

1   Wash and dry the teacup and saucer.

2   Lightly sand the bottom of the teacup. Then sand the top of the saucer. Only sand the middle, where the teacup sits. Sanding helps the glue hold better.

3   Turn the teacup upside down. Apply Weldbond to the part that touches the saucer.

4   Press the teacup firmly onto the saucer. Put a book on top of the cup. This will keep the teacup in place while the Weldbond is drying.

5   It is very important for the Weldbond to dry completely. Check the label and wait as long as it says to.

Continued on the next page

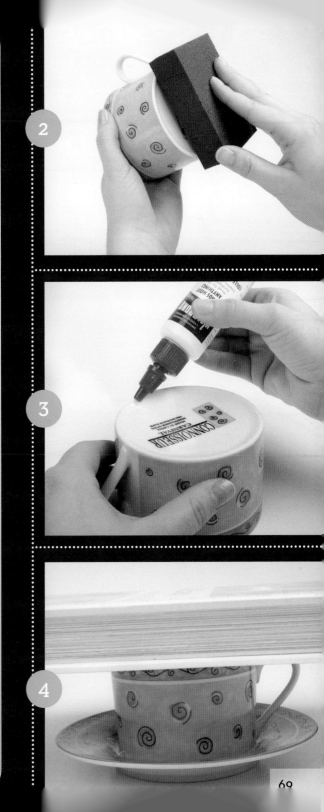

6. Sand the underside of the spoon. Sand the saucer where you want the spoon to sit.

7. Put some Weldbond on the underside of the spoon. Press the spoon firmly in place. Keep pressing for a minute or two. Then let it dry completely.

8. Turn the teacup upside down. Sand a circle in the middle. Make it as big around as the copper pipe and cap.

9   Sand the top of the copper pipe cap. Put glue on the top of the cap.

10 Press the cap to the bottom of the saucer. Wait for the Weldbond to dry completely. Don't do the next step before it is dry.

11 Fill the teacup with birdseed.

12 Stick one end of the copper pipe in the ground. Make sure it won't tip easily. Put the teacup and saucer on top of the pipe using the copper pipe cap.

STUFF YOU'LL NEED

- CERAMIC BOWL

- 2 CERAMIC PLATES, DIFFERENT SIZES

- CERAMIC VASE OR CANDLE HOLDER

- SANDING BLOCK

- WELDBOND

- HEAVY BOOK

CUTE CUPCAKE TIERS

Give old dishes new life!

1   Wash and dry the bowl, plates, and vase.

2   Turn the bowl upside down. Sand the bottom of the bowl. Then put Weldbond on it.

3   Sand the bottom of the larger plate. Put it on the upside-down bowl. Be sure it is centered on the bowl.

4   Put a heavy book on top to hold it down. Let the Weldbond dry completely. Follow the instructions on the label.

5   Sand the bottom of the vase and the center of the plate. Put Weldbond on the bottom of the vase. Place it in the center of the plate. Repeat step 4.

6   Sand the top of the vase and the bottom of the smaller plate. Put Weldbond on the top of the vase. Put the smaller plate on it. Repeat step 4.

7   Use your cupcake tiers to serve cupcakes or other treats!

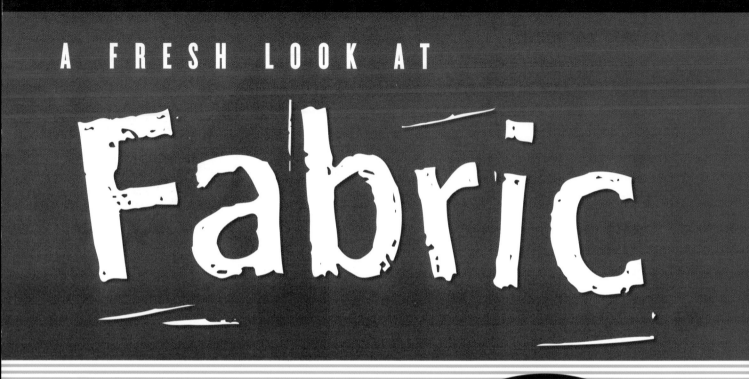

A FRESH LOOK AT
Fabric

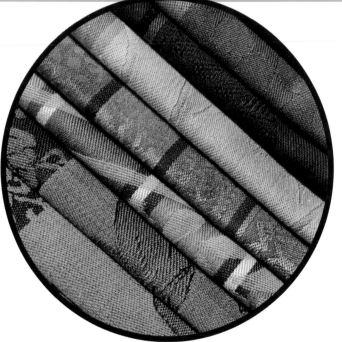

There are many sources for fabric and yarn. Maybe you like to knit, **crochet**, **quilt**, or sew. Or maybe someone you know does. If so, you can use the leftover yarn and fabric scraps. And don't forget about your old clothes. If they can't be **donated**, reuse the material! These things can be upcycled.

THINGS YOU CAN MAKE WITH FABRIC AND YARN SCRAPS

If you can sew, there are many things you can make. The projects in this book require very little sewing.

Yarn scraps can be used in many ways. Old wool sweaters can be made into felt. Crafting with felt is fun and easy too!

Fabric

- PURSES
- BASKETS
- BOOK COVERS
- TOTE BAGS
- GREETING CARDS
- DECORATED SWEATSHIRTS

Yarn

- SCARVES
- HATS
- EARBUD COVERS
- BRACELETS
- CANDLE MATS

WORKING WITH FABRIC

- Wash old clothes before you use them in a craft project.

- If possible, get some fabric scissors. They are made for cutting fabric. They work much better than general-purpose scissors. Don't use them on anything but fabric or they will get dull quickly.

STUFF YOU'LL NEED

- **EARBUDS**
- **MASKING TAPE**
- **YARN SCRAPS**
- **SCISSORS**
- **CRAFT GLUE**

EARBUD WIRE COVERS

Jazz up your earbud wires!

1   Tape the end of the earbud wire to a flat surface. Tie a piece of yarn around the wire near the tape. Tie it with the knot in the middle of the yarn so the ends are even.

2   Bring the left end over the wire. Wrap the right end over the left end and under the wire. Then bring it up between the wire and the left end of the yarn. Pull the knot tight.

3   Now do the opposite. Bring the right end of the yarn over the wire. Wrap the left end over the right end and under the wire. Then bring it up between the wire and the right end of the yarn. Pull the knot tight.

4   Keep repeating steps 2 and 3 until the wire is covered. Add more yarn if necessary. Just tie the new yarn to the ends of the old yarn. Use double knots and cut off the ends close to the knots.

5   When the wire is covered, tie the yarn in a double knot around the wire. Trim the ends. Put a dab of glue on the knot so it won't come undone. Let the glue dry.

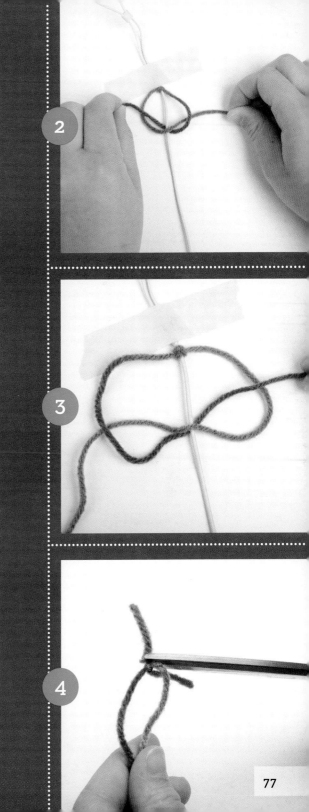

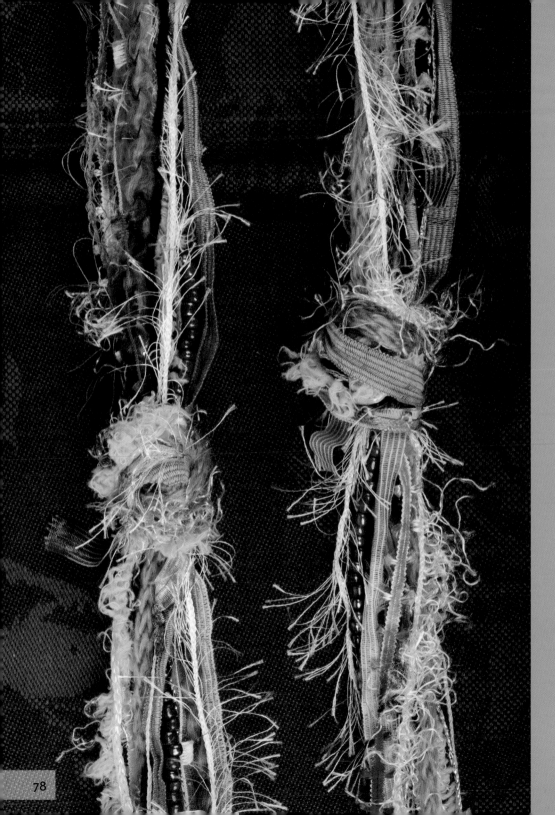

- RULER
- YARN SCRAPS
- SCISSORS
- BEADS
- CLEAR FISHING LINE

FUNKY YARN SCARF

Yarn leftovers made lovely!

1   Decide how long you want the scarf to
     be. Then add 15 inches (38 cm). Cut all of
     the pieces of yarn to the total length.

2   String the beads on the fishing line. Make
     it the same length as the yarn. Tie a knot
     in each end of the fishing line so the
     beads won't fall off.

3   Gather the yarn scraps and the string
     of beads together. Gently twist them to
     make a thick rope. Tie it into a knot in
     the middle.

4   Tie knots about halfway between the
     center and each end. Then tie knots
     about 6 inches (15 cm) from each end.

5   Trim the ends to make them even. Enjoy
     wearing your new scarf!

- ENVELOPE
- CARD STOCK
- DECORATIVE HOLE PUNCHES
- FABRIC SCRAPS
- FABRIC SCISSORS
- SCISSORS
- CRAFT GLUE
- RIBBON
- HEAVY BOOK

FABRIC SCRAP CARD

Give a stack of these as a gift!

1   Fold a piece of card stock in half. Cut it so the card is a little smaller than the envelope. Put the card in the envelope to make sure it fits. Take it back out.

2   Use a decorative hole punch to make holes in the front of the card.

3   Hold the card over different fabric scraps. Find a pattern that looks good through the holes in the card. Cut a piece of fabric that covers the holes. But make sure it doesn't stick out past the edges of the card.

4   Open the card. Put small dots of glue around the holes. Do not use too much glue. Press the fabric over the glue. Cut a piece of card stock to cover the back of the fabric. Glue it over the fabric. Add ribbon or other decorations.

5   Put the card under a heavy book until the glue dries. This keeps the card from warping.

STUFF YOU'LL NEED

- COTTON CLOTHESLINE

- CLEAR TAPE

- SCISSORS

- FABRIC SCRAPS

- FABRIC SCISSORS

- RULER

- WIDE-EYE PLASTIC NEEDLE

- GLUE STICK

- TACKY GLUE

COOL COILED BASKETS

These baskets hold it all!

1. Wrap tape around the end of the clothesline. Cut the cord right at the end of the tape. This keeps the end from **fraying**.

2. Use fabric scissors to cut strips of fabric. They should be 1/2 inch (1.3 cm) wide. Make the strips as long as possible.

3. Put a strip of fabric through the eye of the needle. Pull it through about 2 inches (5 cm).

Continued on the next page

alternate colors

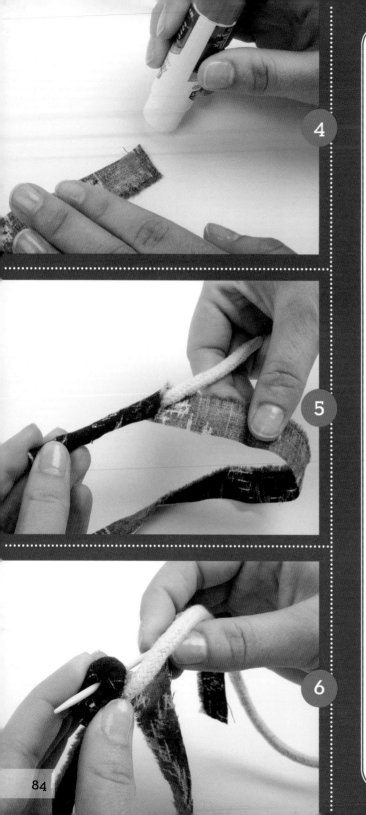

4 Use the glue stick to put glue on the back of the long end of the strip. Cover about 1 inch (2.5 cm) of the strip. Wrap the glued end around the end of the clothesline.

5 Wrap the fabric tightly around the clothesline at an angle. Overlap the edges slightly with each wrap. Cover about 2 inches (5 cm) of the clothesline.

6 Make a tight coil with the wrapped end of the clothesline. Hold it together and put the needle through the center of the coil. Pull the strip all the way through. Pull the fabric tight.

7 Hold the coil tightly. Keep wrapping the fabric around the clothesline. Every inch (2.5 cm) or so, add more of the clothesline to the coil. Attach it by pushing the needle through a gap in the coil. Pull the strip all the way through.

8 When you get to the end of a fabric strip, glue the end around the clothesline. Put another strip on the needle. Glue the end around the clothesline where the previous strip ended.

9 Keep wrapping and coiling. Stop when the coil is as large as you want the bottom of the basket to be.

10 Start creating the sides of the basket. Guide the wrapped clothesline on top of the outer coil instead of next to it. Attach the clothesline like in step 7. Widen the basket by moving each new coil out slightly as you attach it to the previous coil. This takes a bit of practice.

11 To make a handle, pull the wrapped clothesline away from the top coil. Keep it pulled away while attaching the clothesline to the top coil.

12 When the basket is the size you want it, cut the clothesline. Wrap a piece of tape around the end. Use the glue stick to put glue on the end of the fabric strip. Completely cover the end of the clothesline with fabric. Cut off any extra fabric. Glue the end of the clothesline to the basket with Tacky Glue.

85

STUFF YOU'LL NEED

- NEWSPAPER
- BROWN PAPER BAG
- SCISSORS
- MARKER
- STAINED T-SHIRT
- DOUBLE-SIDED TAPE
- FABRIC PAINT
- SMALL BOWL
- WATER
- PAINTBRUSH

PAINT SPLATTER T-SHIRT

Upcycle a stained T-shirt!

1 Spread newspaper over your work surface. If possible, do this activity outside. There will be a lot of splatter!

2 Cut open a brown paper bag. Draw a design to cover the stain on the T-shirt. Poke the scissors through the bag inside the design. Cut from there to the edge of the design. Then cut out the design.

3 Flip the bag over. Put double-sided tape around the edges of the cutout area. Spread the T-shirt out on the newspaper. Turn the bag back over. Place it on the shirt so the stain shows inside the cutout area. Press around the edges of the design. Use more newspaper to cover any part of the shirt that sticks out past the sides of the bag.

4 Put some fabric paint in a bowl. Add a little water to thin the paint. Dip the paintbrush in the paint. Flick the brush toward the cutout area of the bag. Repeat with different colors until the shirt showing through the design is covered with paint. Let the paint dry completely before removing the paper bag.

87

STUFF YOU'LL NEED

- OLD TIE
- RULER
- FABRIC SCISSORS
- WAXED PAPER
- SCISSORS
- TACKY GLUE
- STRAIGHT PINS
- MASKING TAPE
- SELF-ADHESIVE HOOK-AND-LOOP DOTS
- BUTTON, NEEDLE & THREAD (OPTIONAL)

TIE IT, YOU'LL LIKE IT!

Make a pouch for a phone or glasses!

1. Lay the tie out flat. Cut the tie 16 inches (41 cm) from the larger point. Cut off the label. Open the tie by cutting any threads in the center. Cut a piece of waxed paper to fit inside the tie. Glue the tie closed with the waxed paper inside.

2. Put glue along the cut end of the tie. Fold it over about 1 inch (2.5 cm). Pin the fold in place until the glue dries. Remove the pins and waxed paper.

3. Fold the glued end up to where the center seam starts. Put a small piece of masking tape on the table to mark the fold line.

4. Unfold the tie. Make sure not to move it! Put glue along each side from the glued end to the tape mark. Put glue on the glued end too. Fold the tie again and press the edges firmly. Let the glue dry.

5. Put a hook-and-loop dot together. Take the backing off one side. Put the dot near the point of the tie. Remove the backing from the other side. Fold the point to make a flap. Press the dot on top of the end you folded up in step 4. If you want, sew a decorative button on the outside of the flap.

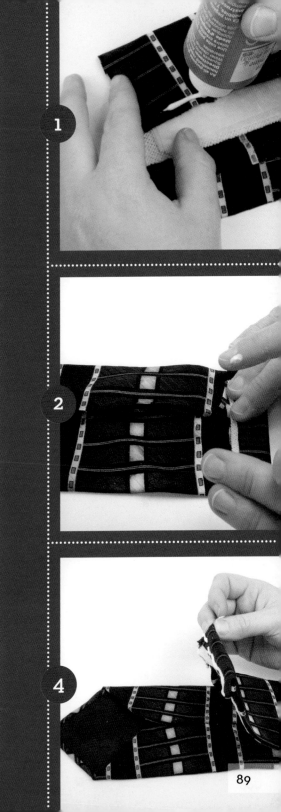

STUFF YOU'LL NEED

- OLD 100% WOOL SWEATER
- MEASURING TAPE
- PAPER
- PEN
- FREEZER PAPER
- MARKER
- RULER
- SCISSORS
- IRON
- FABRIC SCISSORS
- SELF-ADHESIVE HOOK-AND-LOOP DOTS
- EMBROIDERY NEEDLE
- EMBROIDERY FLOSS
- CRAFT FELT (OPTIONAL)
- BUTTON (OPTIONAL)

FELTED WOOL HEADBAND

Give new life to an old sweater!

MAKING FELTED WOOL

Wash the wool sweater in the washing machine using hot water. Then dry it in the dryer using the hottest setting. Check to see if it feels like felt. If it still seems more like woven yarn than felt, wash and dry it again. Repeat until the sweater feels like felt.

1. Wrap the measuring tape around your head as if you were wearing a headband. Add 1 inch (2.5 cm) to the measurement. Write down the total.

2. Tear off a piece of freezer paper. It should be a little longer than the total measurement. Fold it in half crosswise. Draw a straight line from the middle of the fold to the opposite edge.

3. Divide the total measurement in half. Measure that far along the line starting at the fold. Make a mark.

Continued on the next page

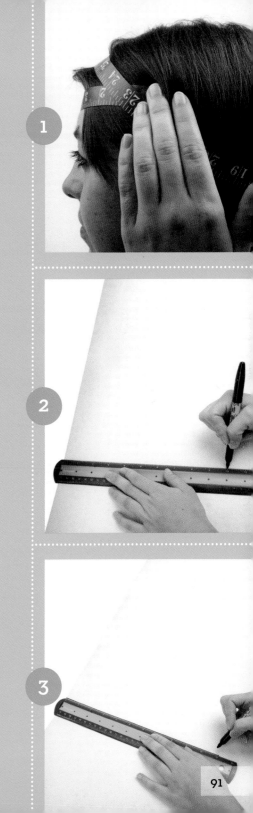

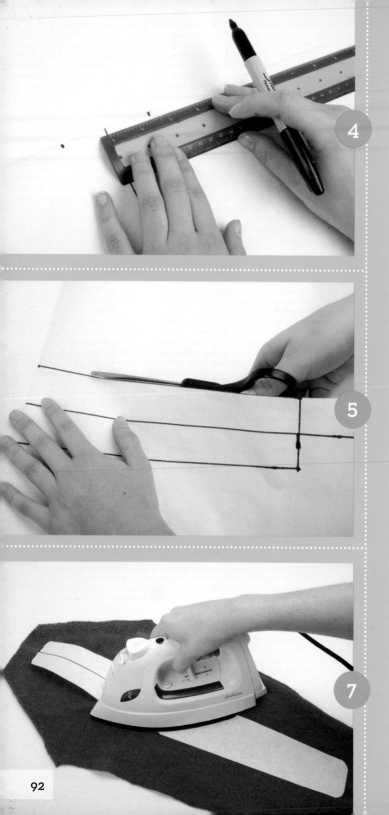

4 Make marks on the fold 1^1/$_2$ inches (4 cm) from each side of the line. Make marks 1 inch (2.5 cm) from each side of the mark you made in step 3.

5 Use a ruler to draw a straight line between the two marks on the right side of the line. Do the same on the left side. Draw a line between the marks that are not on the fold. Cut along the outer lines. Make sure you cut through both layers. Round off the corners on the end away from the fold. Unfold the paper. This is the headband pattern.

6 Wrap the pattern around your head to see if it fits. The ends should **overlap** about 1 inch (2.5 cm). It's okay if it's a little bigger. But if it's too small, make a new pattern using a larger measurement.

7 Place the pattern on the felted wool. Lay it waxy side down. Have an adult help you iron it so it sticks to the felt.

8   Use fabric scissors to cut the felt around the pattern. Remove the pattern. Wrap the felt around your head. Does it fit? Do the ends overlap about 1 inch (2.5 cm)? Is it wider than you want it to be? You can make it smaller by trimming the edges.

9   Put a hook-and-loop dot together. Take the backing off one side. Put it about 1/2 inch (1 cm) from one of the ends. Remove the backing from the other side. Wrap the headband around your head. Press the end with the hook-and-loop dot firmly against the other end.

10   Cut a flower and some leaves out of felt. If you need more colors than you have sweaters, use scraps of craft felt.

11   Use the blanket stitch to sew on the flower and leaves. This stitch is described on the next page. You could also stitch around the edges of the headband. If you want, sew a decorative button over the hook-and-loop dot.

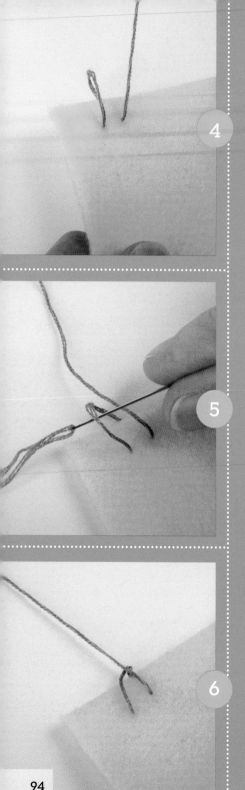

How to do the blanket stitch

The blanket stitch is an embroidery stitch that looks nice on both sides. It is often used around the edges of a project, such as a blanket. You can use floss the same color as the felt. Or choose a different color that will show against the felt.

1   Cut a piece of embroidery floss about 2 feet (61 cm) long. Separate out three strands of floss. *(See opposite page.)*

2   Put the ends of the strands together and thread them through the needle. Pull them about one-quarter of the way through the needle. Tie a knot at the end of the longer side.

3   Position the needle behind the felt about ¼ inch (.6 cm) from the edge. Push the needle up through the felt. Pull it until the knot hits the back of the felt.

4   Move the needle about ¼ inch (.6 cm) to the right of where the thread came up. Push the needle up through the felt again. Pull the floss through most of the way. Leave a little loop.

5   Put the needle through the loop from left to right.

6   Pull it snug.

7   Repeat steps 4 through 6.

8   When you reach the end of the thread or the end of the felt, you'll need to make a knot. Push the needle through the top of the last stitch. Before pulling it all the way, put it through the loop you just made. Pull tight to make a knot.

9   To hide the end, run the needle from the top edge of the felt in about ¼ inch (.6 cm). Pull it through. Cut the thread off right next to the felt.

Separating embroidery floss

There are six strands of thread in embroidery floss. You often need to separate the strands and only use some of them.

1   Roll the end of the floss between your finger and thumb.

2   Separate the ends of the strands.

3   Grasp one strand and gently pull it away from the others. Repeat until you have as many strands as you need.

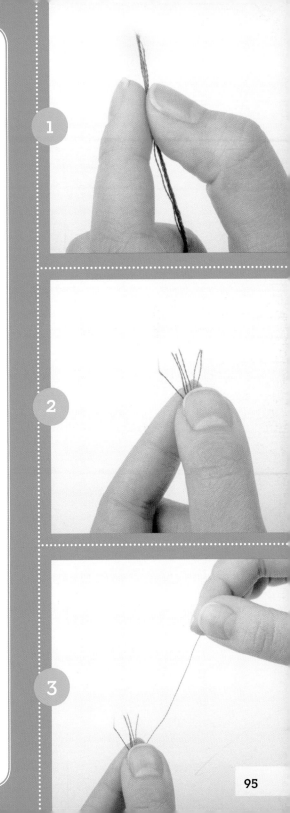

A FRESH LOOK AT

Metal

Many everyday items are made of metal. Metal can be found all around us. It's in cans, license plates, cookie tins, and more. Here are some ideas for reusing or upcycling metal.

Aluminum Cans

Cans come in many sizes. Here are some things they can be made into.

- VASES
- PENCIL HOLDERS
- STORAGE CONTAINERS
- CANDLE HOLDERS

Other Metal Pieces

More than likely you have some unused metal items around your house. You'll find a variety of metal stuff at **garage** sales or secondhand stores. Use your imagination to think of ideas to upcycle those pieces. There are some projects in this book that will get you started.

- MESSAGE TRAY
- DECORATED TIN BOXES
- WIND CHIMES
- HARDWARE ART
- HARDWARE JEWELRY

CLEANING THE METAL

Cans often have labels that must be removed before you reuse them. Some labels come off easily and some take a bit more work. First wash the can in hot, soapy water. Let it dry. If there is still glue on the can, use Goo Gone to remove it. Sometimes it is hard to get off. Just have patience and keep at it. Wash the can again in hot, soapy water. Dry it thoroughly.

STUFF YOU'LL NEED

- **OLD METAL TRAY**
- **SANDING BLOCK**
- **PAINTER'S TAPE**
- **SCISSORS**
- **NEWSPAPER**
- **RUSTY METAL PRIMER**
- **FOAM BRUSH**
- **CHALKBOARD PAINT**
- **WIRE**
- **WIRE CUTTERS**
- **DUCT TAPE**
- **RULER**
- **GLITTER GLUE**
- **DECORATIVE GEMS**

GET THE MESSAGE

Make your own chalkboard!

1. Sand any rust off the surface of the tray.

2. Wash the sanding dust off and dry the tray thoroughly.

3. Put painter's tape around the edge of the tray. Cut slits in the tape to bend it around the corners. Be sure to line up the bottom edges so you have a smooth painting line.

4. If possible, do this step outside. Spread newspaper over your work surface. Paint the tray with rusty metal primer. Follow the directions on the paint can. Let the primer dry completely. Add more coats if needed.

Continued on the next page

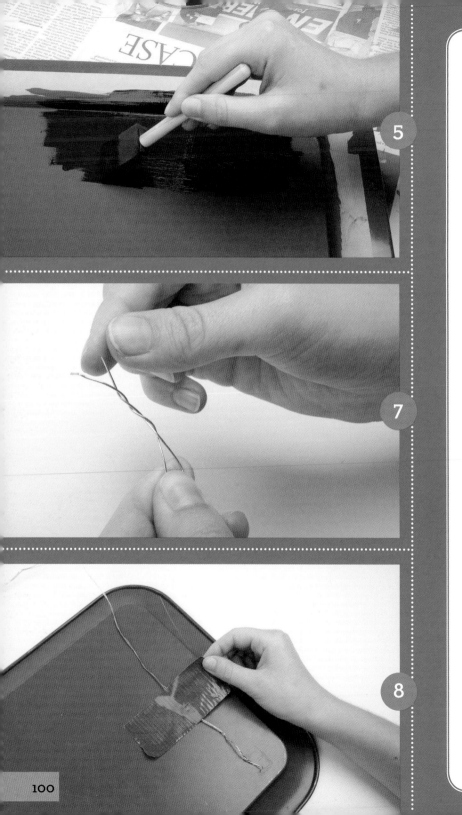

5   Apply the chalkboard paint evenly. Follow the directions on the can. Add more coats if needed. Let it dry completely after each coat.

6   Carefully remove the painter's tape.

7   Cut a piece of wire four times longer than the width of the tray. Fold it in half and twist the halves together.

8   Lay one end along one side of the back of the tray. Put a piece of duct tape over the wire. Leave about 4 inches (10 cm) of wire below the tape.

9   Fold the extra wire up over the duct tape. Twist it tightly around the wire above the duct tape.

10 Repeat steps 8 and 9 to tape the other end of the wire to the other side of the tray.

11 Pull the wire toward the center of the top of the tray. That is the point the tray will hang from. Put a piece of duct tape over the wire about 1 inch (2.5 cm) below the hanging point. This will keep the tray from tilting away from the wall.

12 Decorate the border of the tray. Use glitter glue, gems, or whatever you like.

STUFF YOU'LL NEED

- 7 OR MORE TIN CANS, SAME SIZE
- CRAFT FELT
- FABRIC SCISSORS
- RULER
- MARKER
- CARDBOARD
- SCISSORS
- CRAFT GLUE
- WOODEN SKEWER
- HOT GLUE GUN & GLUE STICKS
- PICTURE HANGERS

TIN CAN ORGANIZER

This storage is totally tubular!

1   Wash the cans thoroughly. Let them dry.

2   Wrap felt around a can. Cut it so the sides just meet.

3   Measure the height of the can. Mark the height on the felt in two places. Draw a line between the marks and cut along the line. Cut more felt rectangles this size. You will need two rectangles for each can. They can be the same color or different colors.

4   Set a can on a piece of cardboard. Trace around the can with a marker. Cut out the circle inside the lines. Make sure the circle fits in the bottom of the can. Cut it smaller if necessary.

Continued on the next page

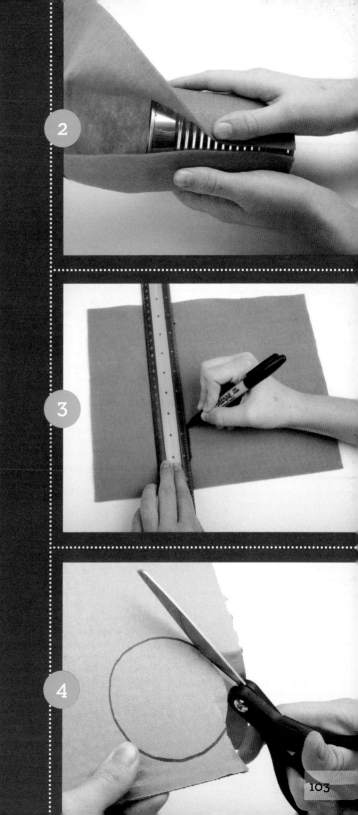

5 Trace around the cardboard circle on a piece of felt. Cut it out. Make sure it fits in the can. Glue it inside the bottom of a can.

6 Put one of the felt rectangles around the inside of the can. If the sides **overlap**, trim them until they meet.

7 Put the felt back in the can. Fold the sides back. Use a wooden skewer to put glue under the felt. Press the sides against the inside of the can.

8 Put glue around the top edges of the can. Press the felt against the can. Smooth out any wrinkles with the clean end of the wooden skewer.

9 Put glue around the edges and in the middle of another felt rectangle.

10   Wrap the felt around the outside of the can. Press the seam together. Add a bit more glue along the seam.

11   Repeat steps 5 through 10 with the other cans. Let the glue dry overnight.

12   Arrange the cans the way you want the organizer to look.

13   Have an adult help you use the hot glue gun. Glue the cans together. Put the glue along the seams in the felt. That way the seams won't show. Be sure to put glue everywhere the cans touch each other.

14   Use hot glue to glue a picture hanger to the bottom of one or two cans. Store your stuff with style!

STUFF YOU'LL NEED

- 2 OLD LICENSE PLATES
- CRAFT FELT
- MARKER
- FABRIC SCISSORS
- HOLE PUNCH
- DOUBLE-SIDED TAPE
- TAG BOARD
- SCISSORS
- PAPER
- 2 LOOSE-LEAF BOOK RINGS

LICENSE TO WRITE

Car not included!

1. Wash and dry the license plates. Set a license plate on the felt. Trace around it with a marker. Make dots where the top two holes are. Cut out the felt just inside the marker line. Punch out the holes. Cut a second piece of felt the same way.

2. Put double-sided tape all around the edges of the back of each license plate. Put some in the middle too. Stick a piece of felt to each license plate.

3. Cut a piece of tag board a little smaller than the license plates. Cut a second piece of tag board and a bunch of paper the same size.

4. Put one of the tag board rectangles under a license plate. Make it even with the top edge. Center it between the sides of the license plate. Make marks where the holes are. Punch the holes out of the tag board.

5. Use the tag board as a **template** to punch holes in the same places on the other tag board rectangle and the sheets of paper.

6. Put the paper between the tag board rectangles. Put a license plate on each side. Attach a book ring through each hole.

- OLD TIN BOX
- PAINTER'S TAPE
- NEWSPAPER
- SPARKLE MOD PODGE
- SMALL PAINTBRUSH
- GLITTER
- CRAFT KNIFE (OPTIONAL)
- FOAM BRUSH

GLITTERY BOX

Storage space in a cool case!

1. Take the lid off the box. Use painter's tape to cover the top edge of the box where the lid sits. You don't want to put any glitter there.

2. You will apply the glitter one color at a time. Put tape around the areas where you want to put the first color of glitter. Smooth the edges with your fingernail so they are tight against the box.

3. Put tape over the rim of the lid. Then tape around the areas on the lid where you want to put the first color of glitter.

Continued on the next page

4 Spread newspaper over your work area. Use a small paintbrush to put Sparkle Mod Podge inside the taped areas on the box. Sprinkle the first color of glitter over the Mod Podge. Make sure the area is covered completely. Gently tap the box to knock off the extra glitter. If you missed any spots, just add a little more Mod Podge and glitter. Tap off the extra.

5 Repeat step 4 on the lid. Brush the exposed areas of the lid with Mod Podge. Add glitter and gently tap off the extra. Let both pieces dry completely. Pour the extra glitter from the newspaper back into its container.

6 Once the Mod Podge is completely dry, carefully remove the tape. You may want to use a craft knife to cut along the edge of the tape for a smooth line. Leave the tape on the edges of the box and lid.

7. Put tape around the areas where you want to put the next color of glitter. You don't need to put tape where there is already glitter. The glitter forms a border for the other colors. Brush on Mod Podge. Be careful not to put any on the dry glitter. Add the next color of glitter and tap off the extra. Let it dry completely.

8. Repeat steps 6 and 7 until the box and lid are covered with glitter. Let it dry completely.

9. Remove the tape from the edges of the box and lid. Use a foam brush to cover the box and lid with one or two coats of Sparkle Mod Podge. Let it dry completely after each coat.

- SODA CAN TABS
- FLAT-NOSED PLIERS
- COLORED WIRE (22 GAUGE)
- WIRE CUTTERS
- RULER
- HEAD PINS
- SMALL BEADS
- ROUND-NOSED PLIERS
- EAR WIRES
- COLORED JUMP RINGS

CAN TAB EARRINGS

Mix and match!

1. If any of the tabs still have the flap where they were attached to the can, use a flat-nosed pliers to remove them.

2. Cut two pieces of colored wire about 3 inches (8 cm) long.

3. Wrap both wires around the thinner loop on a tab. Put one wire on each side of the loop.

4. There will be a gap between the wires. Use a flat-nosed pliers to press the ends down so they don't stick out.

Continued on the next page

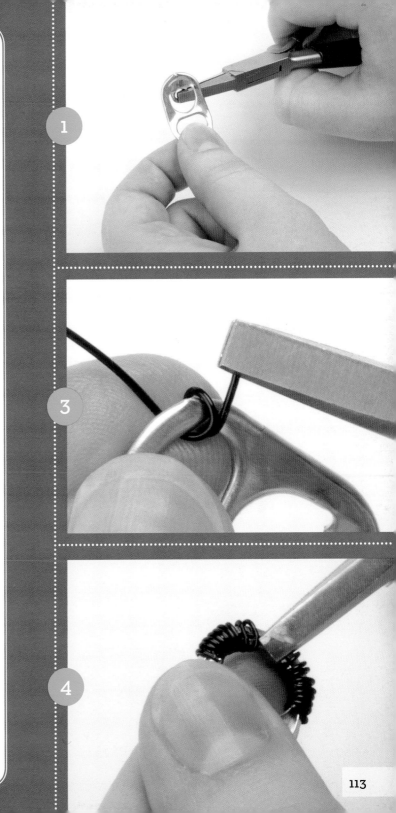

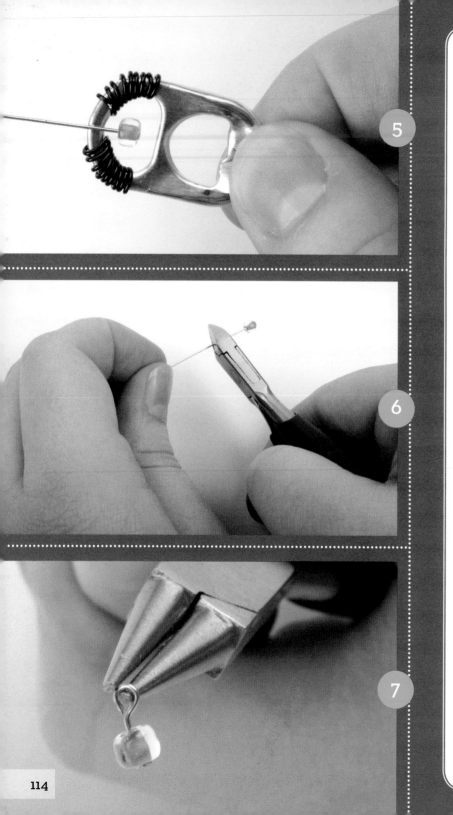

5   Put a small bead on a
    head pin. Make sure
    the bead fits inside the
    loop you wrapped the
    wires around.

6   Use the wire cutters to
    trim the head pin wire.
    Cut it about 1/4 inch
    (.6 cm) from the bead.

7   Use the round-nosed
    pliers to make a loop
    in the head pin wire
    above the bead. Bend
    the wire to one side.
    Then grab the end
    of the wire with the
    pliers and twist to
    form a loop. Use the
    pliers to close the gap
    if needed.

8. Use the pliers to twist open the ring of an ear wire. Hang the bead on the ear wire by the loop you made.

9. Put the ear wire ring around the can tab between the colored wire. Close the ring on the ear wire with the pliers.

10. Use the flat-nosed pliers to gently open the colored jump rings. Hold one side and use the pliers to twist one end to the side. Do not pull the ends away from each other. Put the rings on the other loop of the can tab. Close the rings.

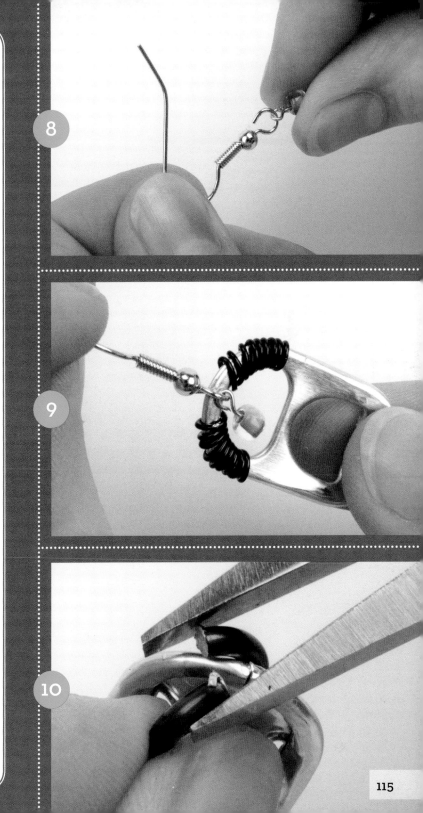

- RIBBON

- RULER

- SCISSORS

- GLUE STICK

- GRILL

- HOT GLUE GUN
  & GLUE STICKS

- 4 WOODEN
  BEADS

- PAPER CLIP

EaRRING GRILL

Show off your earrings on the grill!

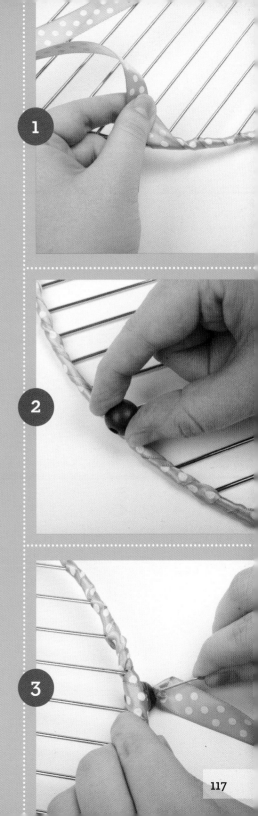

1. Cut a piece of ribbon about 36 inches (91 cm) long. Use the glue stick to put some glue on the end. Wrap the ribbon around the rim of the **grill**. Secure the end with glue. Cut more ribbon and repeat until the entire rim is covered.

2. Have an adult help you use the hot glue gun. Glue the beads to the back of the grill. Spread them out evenly around the rim. Place the beads with the holes pointing out to the side. Let the glue dry.

3. Cut four pieces of ribbon about 18 inches (46 cm) long. Unfold a paper clip and use it to push a ribbon through each bead. Bring the ends of each ribbon around the rim and tie them into bows.

4. Cut another ribbon about 36 inches (91 cm) long. Fold it in half. Put the ends between the top two grill wires from back to front. One end should be on each side of the center wire. Hold the middle of the ribbon above the rim of the grill. Bring the ends of the ribbon over the rim and through the loop made by the middle of the ribbon. Pull it tight. Tie the ends together. Hang up the grill and add your earrings!

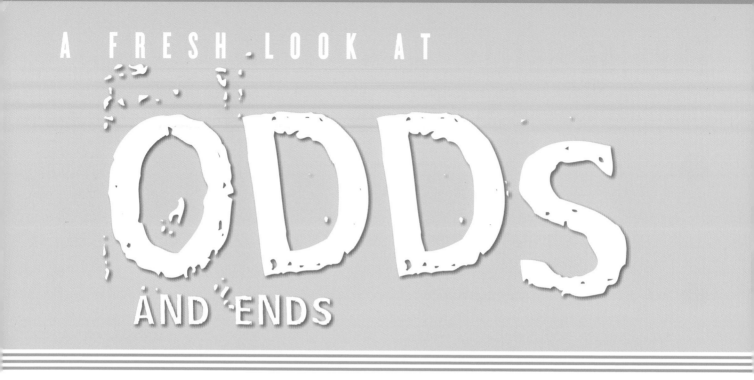

A FRESH LOOK AT ODDS AND ENDS

What exactly are odds and ends? The dictionary defines them as miscellaneous small items, remnants, or leftovers. How about that old coffee table that is scratched and has a broken leg? What about old toys you have lying around? Bits of furniture, paper, hardware, and plastic can be turned into some really cool things. Don't trash them, create with them!

Project Materials

Here is a list of things that could be used in upcycling projects. Think before you throw something away or recycle it. You can find ideas for upcycling almost anything. Try looking online for different projects you'd like to do.

- GAME PIECES
- PICTURE FRAMES
- METAL SCREENS
- BOWLING BALLS
- USED CDs OR DVDs
- PENCILS
- FURNITURE
- KITCHEN UTENSILS
- TIN BOXES
- OLD WINDOWS
- HARDWARE
- LEFTOVER BEADS

STUFF YOU'LL NEED

- OLD FRAME WITH GLASS
- NEWSPAPER
- PAINTBRUSH
- ACRYLIC PAINT
- ACRYLIC SEALER
- 4 LARGE WOODEN BEADS
- WOODEN SKEWER
- PAINT PENS
- MARKER
- DECORATIVE PAPER
- SCISSORS
- CARDBOARD (OPTIONAL)
- PLIERS
- CRAFT GLUE
- HOT GLUE GUN & GLUE STICKS

FUNKY DRESSER TRAY

Keep your baubles on this beauty!

1. Remove the backing and glass from the frame. If the backing has a stand, remove it. Just bend it back and forth until it comes off.

2. Spread newspaper over your work surface. Paint one side of the frame white. Let the paint dry. Then paint the other side white. Let the paint dry.

3. Choose a color for the frame. Paint it with a few coats of that color paint. Let the paint dry after each coat. Finally, add a coat of acrylic sealer.

4. Put the beads on the skewer. Paint the beads to match the frame. You may need to use a couple of coats. Let the paint dry after each coat. Use paint pens to decorate the beads. Apply acrylic sealer. Let it dry.

Continued on the next page

5. Trace around the glass on a piece of decorative paper. Cut it out.

6. Clean both sides of the glass. Put the glass back in the frame. Put the decorative paper face down on the glass.

7. Put the frame backing on the decorative paper. If it is loose, put some cardboard under it so it fits tightly.

Everything from photos to wallpaper can be used as decorative paper. Try using leftover wrapping paper or scrapbooking paper.

8. Secure the backing. Most frames have tabs that you push down onto the backing.

9. Cut another piece of decorative paper 1/4 inch (.6 cm) smaller than the frame. Put a thin line of glue around the edge of the paper. Press it onto the back of the frame. Let the glue dry.

10. Have an adult help you use the hot glue gun. Glue a bead to each corner of the frame. Let the glue dry.

11. Flip the tray over and set it on your dresser. Arrange your favorite **accessories** on it!

STUFF YOU'LL NEED

- LARGE BASKET WITH HANDLE

- MEASURING TAPE

- FABRIC

- FABRIC SCISSORS

- PILLOW STUFFING

- SELF-ADHESIVE HOOK-AND-LOOP TAPE

- SCISSORS

- SAFETY PINS

- CRAFT FELT

- POM-POMS

- TAPESTRY NEEDLE

- STRETCHY STRING

- JINGLE BELLS

COOL KITTY BED

For first-class felines!

1. Measure the inside of the basket. Choose the fabric for the pillow. It should be 2¹/₂ times longer and 10 inches (25 cm) wider than the basket.

2. Fill the bottom of the basket with pillow stuffing. Shape it into a pillow. Use enough stuffing to make it firm.

3. Cut a 4-inch (10 cm) strip of the hook-and-loop tape. Lay the fabric out face down. Take the stuffing out of the basket. Set it in the middle of the fabric. Wrap the fabric around the stuffing. Remove the backing from one side of the hook-and-loop tape. Stick it to the fabric where it overlaps. Remove the backing from the other side of the hook-and-loop tape. Press the edge of the fabric onto it.

Continued on the next page

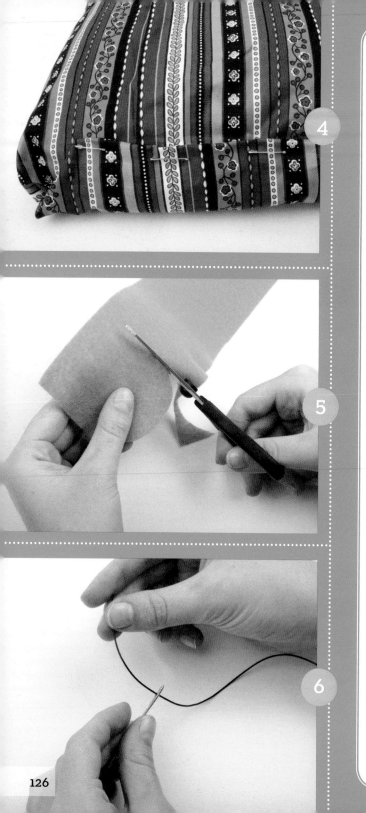

4 Fold the sides of the fabric around the stuffing like you would wrap a present. Pin the sides with safety pins. Turn the pillow over and put it in the basket. If the basket is round, turn the corners under so it fits in the basket. Just undo the fabric when you want to wash it.

5 Now make some hanging cat toys! Cut five fun shapes out of felt. Try circles, triangles, squares, or rectangles. Use different colors. The shapes should be a little bigger than the pom-poms.

6 Cut a piece of stretchy string about 24 inches (61 cm) long. Put one end of the string through the tapestry needle. Pull it through about 6 inches (15 cm).

7   Push the needle through the center of a pom-pom. Then through a piece of felt. Repeat to add the rest of the pom-poms and felt shapes.

8   Push the needle through the loop at the top of a jingle bell.

9   Push the needle back through all the felt and pom-poms. Remove the needle. Tie the ends of the string in a double knot close to the first pom-pom.

10 Separate the ends of the string. Tie them around the handle of the basket. Tie several knots. Cut off the extra string. Repeat steps 5 through 9 if you want to make more cat toys to hang on the basket.

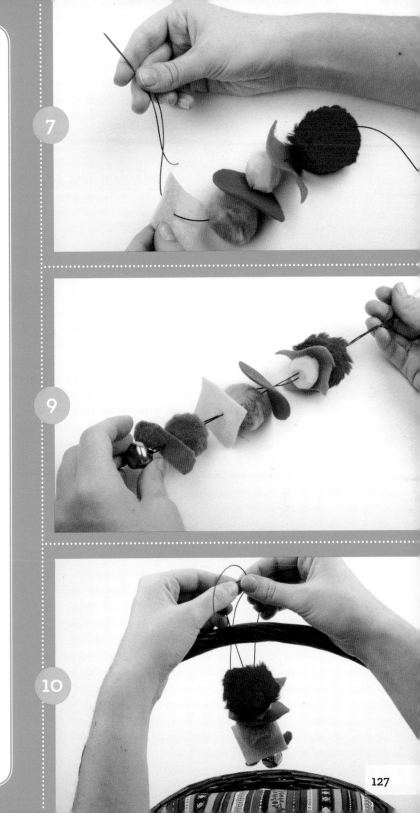

STUFF YOU'LL NEED

- **STURDY STAND**

- **BOWLING BALL**

- **ISOPROPYL ALCOHOL**

- **PAPER TOWELS**

- **ALL-PURPOSE PERMANENT ADHESIVE**

- **COLORFUL FLAT MARBLES**

GORGEOUS GAZING BALL

Add a bright spot to your garden!

1. Find a stand that will hold the bowling ball. It could be an old metal plant stand, a stand for a vase, or even an old coffee can.

2. Place the bowling ball on the stand. Clean it thoroughly with isopropyl alcohol and paper towels.

3. Put a thin layer of adhesive on a small area of the ball.

4. Press a marble into the adhesive. Pull it back a little bit and press it onto the ball again. Do this two or three times. Then press and hold it until it stays in place. This will help the marble stick to the ball better.

5. Repeat steps 3 and 4 until the ball is completely covered with marbles.

6. The marbles will make the gazing ball very heavy. Ask an adult to help you put it in the perfect spot!

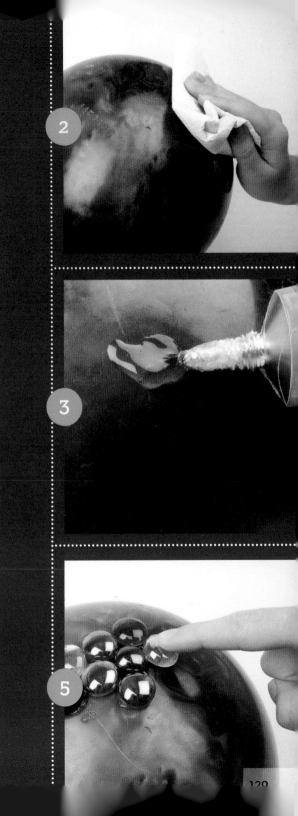

- OLD PENCILS

- PENCIL SHARPENER

- OLD WOODEN RULER

- HOT GLUE GUN & GLUE STICKS

- PICTURE HANGER

PENCIL ART

Do the write thing!

1   Sharpen the pencils until they are the length you want them to be.

2   Lay the pencils out side by side. Make sure any writing on the pencils is facing the same way.

3   Lay the ruler face up on a flat surface. Have an adult help you use the hot glue gun. Put two 2-inch (5 cm) lines of hot glue on the ruler.

4   Press the pencils into the glue while it is still hot. Add more glue as necessary. Keep adding pencils until the ruler is completely covered.

5   Glue a picture hanger to the back of the ruler. Find a place to hang your art!

131

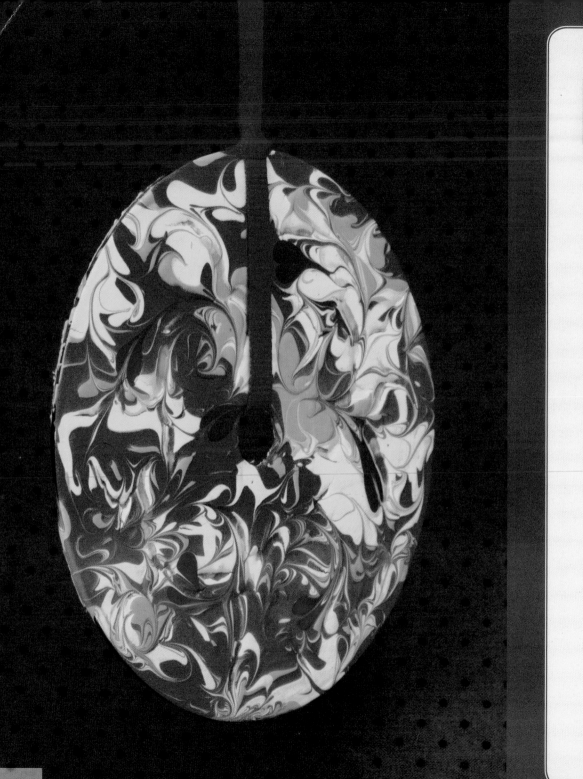

STUFF YOU'LL NEED

- OLD CD
- DOUBLE-SIDED TAPE
- PAPER PLATE
- ACRYLIC PAINT
- WOODEN SKEWER
- ACRYLIC SEALER
- CRAFT KNIFE
- RIBBON

SWIRLY CD ART

An artistic way to upcycle CDs!

1   Put a couple of pieces of double-sided tape on the back of the CD. Stick it to the center of a paper plate.

2   Put some paint on the CD. Use at least three colors. Try not to get the paint too thick, but cover the surface of the CD.

3   Use a wooden skewer to make swirls in the paint. Be careful not to overdo it or the colors will blend together too much. Let the paint dry for at least 8 to 10 hours.

4   Put a coat of acrylic sealer over the dried paint. You may see some cracks in the paint. That's okay. Just fill them with sealer. Let the sealer dry.

5   Use a craft knife to cut around the edges and the center of the CD. Then lift it from the plate.

6   Tie a ribbon through the center hole and hang it up!

- OLD DOMINOES AND/OR SCRABBLE TILES

- DECORATIVE PAPER

- MARKER

- SCISSORS

- MOD PODGE

- PAINTBRUSH

- MOD PODGE DIMENSIONAL MAGIC

- GLUE-ON BAILS

- ALL-PURPOSE PERMANENT ADHESIVE

- CHAINS

- HANG RINGS & EAR WIRES

- PLIERS

Game Piece Jewelry

No playing games with this jewelry!

1   Set a game piece on decorative paper. Trace around it. Cut the shape out inside the lines. Trim the edges as needed to fit the game piece.

2   Brush Mod Podge on the game piece and on the back of the decorative paper. Stick the paper to the game piece. Smooth out the wrinkles.

3   Put a coat of Mod Podge on the sides and top of the game piece. Let the Mod Podge dry.

4   Cover the decorated side of the game piece with Dimensional Magic. Apply it very slowly. Try to avoid getting any bubbles in it. Pop any bubbles that appear right away. Be sure to cover the game piece all the way to the edge. Let it dry at least 8 to 10 hours.

5   Use permanent adhesive to glue a bail to the back. Let the glue dry and then hang it on a chain. For earrings, glue a hang ring to the back of each game piece. Let the glue dry and then use pliers to attach them to ear wires.

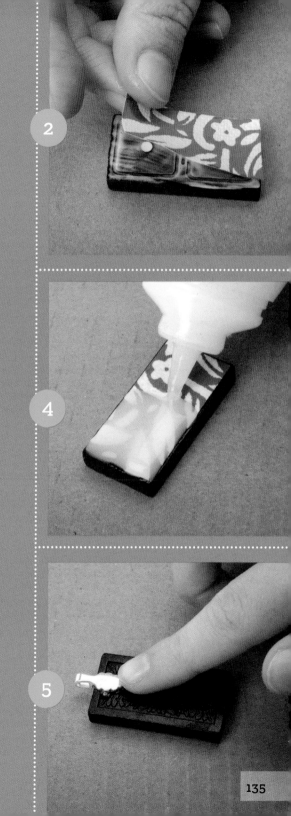

STUFF YOU'LL NEED

- MARKER
- PAPER
- RULER
- SCISSORS
- DOUBLE-SIDED TAPE
- OLD METAL SCREEN
- PLIERS
- WAXED PAPER
- GLITTER GLUE
- DECORATIVE GEMS
- BEADS, DIFFERENT SIZES
- THIN, FLEXIBLE WIRE
- COLORED WIRE (OPTIONAL)

SUPER SCREEN SAVERS

Make your old screens fly!

1 Draw the shape of dragonfly wings on paper. The wings need to be one piece that is narrow in the middle. Draw a line around the outside of the wing shape 1/4 inch (.6 cm) away. Cut around the outer line.

2 Use double-sided tape to attach the paper wings to a piece of screen. Cut out the wings. Carefully move the paper wings to another piece of screen. Cut out a second set of wings.

3 Use a pliers to fold the edges of the wings over 1/4 inch (.6 cm) all the way around. Press the edges flat with the pliers. Be careful! The screen can poke your skin. Turn the wings over and trim any stray wires with a scissors.

4 Set the wings on a piece of waxed paper. Attach decorative gems to the wings with glitter glue. Use quite a bit of glue, since some of it will go through the screen.

Continued on the next page

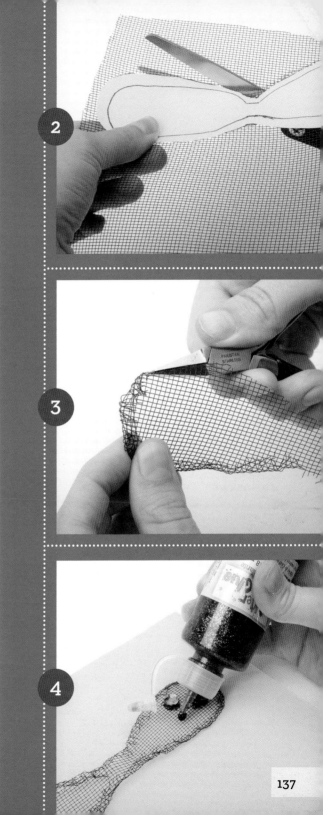

137

5　Put a line of glitter glue around the edges of the wings. Move the wings to a clean piece of waxed paper. Let them dry completely. Then turn the wings over and add a drop of glitter glue behind each gem. Let it dry.

6　Cut a piece of wire about 24 inches (61 cm) long. Put a bead on the wire. Then add a smaller bead. Bring about 10 inches (25 cm) of the wire through the beads. Then thread the wire back through the large bead, but not the small bead. Pull it snug. This is the dragonfly's head.

7　Cut a piece of wire about 4 inches (10 cm) long for the antennae. Use colored wire if you have it. Push one end through the small bead toward the large bead. Push about half of the wire through the small bead. Wrap the antennae wire around the wire between the two beads. Then push the antennae wire back up through the small bead. Curl the ends of the antennae with a pliers.

8 Choose a long, narrow bead for the body. Put one of the wires from the head through the body bead. Add more smaller beads to make the tail.

9 Stop adding beads when there is about 2 inches (5 cm) of wire left. Push the end of the wire back through the next-to-last bead. Use pliers to pull it tight. Wrap the end of the wire around the last few tail beads.

10 Cross the wings over each other at their middles. Hold them against the body bead. Wrap the other wire from the head around the wings and around both ends of the body bead. Make sure the wire holds the wings on securely. Cut off any extra wire.

11 Cut a pice of wire about 3 inches (7.6 cm) long. Wrap it between the head and body. Make sure the ends are even. The ends can be legs if you set the dragonfly on a shelf. Or you can use them to hang the dragonfly on a window screen.

139

GLOSSARY

ACCESSORY – an article of jewelry or clothing that adds completeness or attractiveness to an outfit.

ACCORDION – folded back and forth like the sides of an accordion.

ADHESIVE – something used to stick things to each other.

ATTIC – a room right under the roof of a building.

AVAILABLE – able to be had or used.

CANVAS – a piece of cloth that is stretched over a frame and used as a surface for a painting.

CERAMIC – something made out of clay that is baked at high temperatures to become very hard.

COMBINATION – two or more things put together in a certain way.

CORK – a material made out of tree bark.

CROCHET – to use a special needle with a hook to weave things out of yarn or thread.

CRUMPLE – to crush or bend something out of shape.

DEFINE – to give the meaning of a word.

DESCRIBE – to tell about something with words or pictures.

DIAGONAL – from one corner of a square or rectangle to the opposite corner.

DISCARD – to throw away.

DONATE – to give a gift in order to help others.

FRAY – to unravel or become worn at the edge.

GARAGE – a room or building that cars are kept in. A *garage sale* is a sale that takes place in a garage.

GRILL – a device with parallel metal bars on which food is cooked.

HARDWARE – metal tools and supplies used to build things.

LENGTHWISE – in the direction of the longest side.

ORIGAMI – the Japanese art of paper folding.

OVERLAP – to lie partly on top of something.

MISCELLANEOUS – of different kinds.

NECKLACE – a decoration that is worn around the neck.

OPTION – something you can choose.

PERMISSION – when a person in charge says it's okay to do something.

PRY – to separate two things by sticking something between them and pushing them apart.

QUILT - to sew a blanket that has two layers of cloth with a warm filling such as wool or cotton in the middle.

REMNANT - a small bit that remains after the rest is gone.

SCARF - a long piece of cloth worn around the neck for decoration or to keep warm.

SCORE - to mark with a line or scratch.

SHELF - a thin, flat surface used to store things.

SPLATTER - drops of liquid that have been thrown or scattered around.

STACK - 1. a pile of things placed one on top of the other. 2. to put things in a pile.

STITCH - a small length of thread left in fabric by moving the needle in and out one time.

SWIRL - to whirl or to move smoothly in circles.

TEMPLATE - a shape you draw or cut around to copy it onto something else.

THRIFT STORE - a store that sells used items, especially one that is run by a charity.

TIER - one of two or more rows, layers, or levels.

TOWEL - a cloth or paper used for cleaning or drying.

VENTILATION - the movement of air through a room or other space.

Web sites

To learn more about cool craft projects, visit ABDO Publishing Company on the World Wide Web at www.abdopublishing.com. Web sites about creative ways for upcycling trash are featured on our Book Links page. These links are routinely monitored and updated to provide the most current information available.

INDEX